MICHAEL GRABER

GOING

Electric

TALES OF INNOVATION

from where

Rock'n'Roll was born

"Michael is a innovation practitioner and visionary.
He is a poet who is wildly imaginative, yet a profoundly
pragmatic thinker, an authentic Creative Professional. "

—

Jay Morgan, Global VP Innovation, Bayer Consumer Care

For information, contact Nautilus Publishing, 426 S. Lamar Blvd., Suite 16, Oxford, MS 38655

ISBN: 978-1-936946-67-9

First Edition

Library of Congress Cataloging-in-Publication Data has been applied for.
Printed in the United States of America

10   9   8   7   6   5   4   3   2   1

PREFACE

Dear reader, this book archives many of the articles written for a variety of publications since the Southern Growth Studio began nine years ago. Thanks to *Innovation Excellence, Memphis Daily News, GE Idea Labs, Interactions, and Upstart Business Journals* for first commissioning and publishing the pieces.

Writing a weekly article allows me to articulate and externalize many of the issues that arise during the workweek—and I hope you find value in these trench-inspired insights. You may notice two things:

1). Innovation, the word, is brought up too many times. Many of the pieces are a response to different interpretations of this word and how it impacts a project or culture. Now, in hindsight, I define the word as changing a culture and its methods for creating new value, I have wrestled with this definition for years, a lover's quarrel, and you have a front-row seat.

2). The way you read this book is up to you. As a collection of pieces, you don't have to read in sequence. You may find an essay to match a particular issue. This book is your resource. Play with it.

Lastly, the Southern Growth Studio has the opportunity to work with leading global clients in Healthcare, Consumer Goods, Logistics, Electronics, Durable Goods, Software, Sports, Hospitality, and with Cities and Non-Profits. To protect their trade secrets we do not name them, save for rare cases. Thanks to all clients, Studio Members (past and present), and our families. Thanks, too, to my founding co-partner who left the Studio to run one of our ventures, Jocelyn Atkinson. Many of her ideas and phrases pepper this book, as she is a burning-bright professional and great friend.

Hope you find insights you can use and inspiration here.

Michael Graber
Founder & Managing Partner of Southern Growth Studio

PREAMBLE

Once Upon a Time, at Work.

In business and daily life, we are wired for stories as a species. One creation myth begins by saying God created humans because he needed good stories. Stories bind us together, creating an emotionally connected narrative through which we make sense of the world. I want to share a *Here's What I Love About My Career* story with you.

The background is a co-creation session where we were exploring grooming products. The third group consisted of Extreme Men, masculine dudes: Iron men, Paratroopers, Special Forces, and one stereotypical Hipster. From his wave-like, flowing beard to his shaved head and skullcap, this Hipster was the rouge element in the session. He reeked of marijuana, was a few minutes late, and made sure to point out many of his tattoos. He also talked about his job a lot, a clerk in a Vape store.

As we worked through concepts and conversation, he was quick to proclaim his Hipster creed. For example, he rebelled vehemently against anything that required recharging or refilling, preferring the virtues of a straight razor and shaving foam. This quest for authenticity was not shared by the others, who valued efficiency, a rewarding sensory experience, and convenience. After saying "thank you for the social theory, but please do not assume your view of reality is reality for everyone else in the room" and respectfully stopping his monologue, we moved to the next concept.

Without missing a beat, he emoted, "Now, this one, this one is something I'd love!" He continued, "guys, I have a confession to make. I have a hairy back and this would make it much easier for me to reach." Then he shared something so endearing, it softened the hearts of hardened men: "My mom used to shave it for me. Now, my girlfriend does."

One of the special forces members stood up, banged once on the table, pointed, and praised: "she's a keeper!" The room broke out in spontaneous applause.

This very human story serves as a testament to the innate power of people to support and encourage one another. At this moment I squealed like a happy pig. Joy infused the air. Wisdom was being shared from one tribe to another. Bonds were forming. Kindness was overflowing. In a nanosecond, a contemplative instinct rang out and a voice broke within: *"what a blessing and honor to do this work."* At root, the session wasn't about the product concepts, but humanity's essential unity. One subject was just a means to getting through the illusory veil of separateness.

Then, the analytical side of me tapped its imaginary pencil on the conference room table, indicating that it was time to get back to work, tally up the votes on the concept, foster conversation around what changes my new friends would make to the prototype, and lead a discussion around pricing.

Stories are the taproot of humanity. They define culture. What stories are you gathering and sharing at your business? How do they transform you personally and your organization for the better?

How to Define Innovation?
Word. Culture. Mindset.

The New Era of Human-to-Human Business

Finding a Better Word for Innovation.

Remember when the word "paradigm" was killed in the dot-com era? How about "synergy" "edgy" or the prefix "e-" – these expressions all died from the same disease: overuse.

Now, the word "innovation" has been uttered so many times that it has lost its breath, meaning, and resonance.

A quick glance at death by burnout: there were 33,528 mentions of "innovation" in quarterly and annual reports last year alone; 255 new books published in one recent 90-day period had "innovation" in the title.

According to a recent Cap Gemini study, four in 10 executives claim to be a chief innovation officer. Yet the findings show a dark side. Most of the executives interviewed admit that the title is "for appearances" and that there is not a clear strategy for their innovation efforts.

A consulting industry now exists to aid innovation efforts, with project costs ranging from $30,000 to $1 million.

Even business schools try to squeeze life out of the tired phrase – 28 percent of them note "innovation" in their mission statements alone.

In plain language, the word "innovation" has been hijacked by the unimaginative, the posers, and the lemmings of the business community.

While scholars split hairs about the various types of innovations, the mere fact that they are arguing the topic means that it's dead.

Leading companies define the market. They define the market by following a process that recreates market expectations, creating a leadership position. Meaning gets created by the language used to describe this naturally occurring process with companies who strive to grow.

Then, the problem starts. All the followers use the language of the few leaders, because they lack the will to create in the first place. It's sickening, really. Language creates meaning and expectations – and the world of business understands this basic human truth less than most other fields.

Readers, can we make a deal? Can we create a movement? Can we redefine "innovation?" It used to be such a strong word, but has been watered down to the point of meaninglessness.

What is the thrust behind this word, anyway?

Where we work, we define it as Strategic Growth. Yet, other concepts could always fill the void.

How about Value Generation? Is that what is at stake?

Invention? Or is this too imbued with overtones of mystical pseudo science?

Smart Business? Planning? Market foresight? Trend creation?

Help. Innovation has died from exhaustion, overuse, and misuse. Innovation, as a label, has died.

Business continues. Welcome to the creative process. Lead. Name it yourself.

Long live _____.

Culture is The Key
Indicator of Innovation

An odd dynamic is taking place among the C-suite of many companies. They demand more innovation from the organization without really knowing what that means and the implications it has for the organization.

Innovation requires a change in the organization, but leaders are too often unwilling to do what is required to make the changes.

When an organization needs more innovation, it needs to first prime the culture. Start by getting a team ready with exercises, such as meeting with customers, going into the field, or brain-activating exercises.

The second element is working on the culture itself. Otherwise, there will be conflict. When a team has a full portfolio of potential gold for the company and the culture is not ready to receive it, bad will is created.

The hard work is getting the culture ready to receive this change in behavior, mindset and their existing business model.

What you find is the rise of the cultural antibodies. They attack this team and their ideas like a foreign object that entered a body. They suppress the new concepts as quickly as possible. This is a telltale sign that the culture needs to be worked on before commissioning an innovation project.

To begin considering a change in culture, one activity asks the senior leadership team to examine new models of revenue. This helps to push the team in new directions and can also identify revenue opportunities that are easily attainable.

Such cultural change activities help the organization to understand what exists, what can be changed and what is essential. Organizations frequently find that what they thought was impossible is actually within reach.

Organizations seeking to improve their innovation culture need three things:

1. The full support and backing of the executive team in ways that are visible to the organization.

2. Building multidisciplinary innovation teams that understand how to lead innovation efforts.

3. These teams then help others in the organization, being sherpas to show methods, teach and walk alongside those learning the new techniques.

Culture is the actions taken or not taken.

To begin an innovation discipline, every organization needs to set aside some time to figure out what they are willing to become. They need to figure out if they are willing to change their behavior to achieve a desirable outcome.

For example, if you're a product company and you have rising costs, and your returns are negligible or declining, you probably need to change the way you're creating and designing products. Before making these changes, change the culture. Or *else*.

When Did We Stop New Thinking?

Human evolution is a complex topic. Personal growth may be more perplexing even to the best psychologists. The theme that really defies reason is when a whole organization or market segment falls into the trap of formal rigidity, as in "it's just the way it is."

Accepting life as it is, accepting your job as it is, accepting the function of an organization as it exists today is not only lazy but dangerous.

Life, work cultures, the market and technology are too dynamic to be thought of in absolute and fixed terms. This unprecedented rate of change calls for humans to be wholly present, aware and adaptive.

Sure, it's critically important to begin by deeply and critically understanding a snapshot of the mental model of today's reality; however, that is just a first step. Exploring new models of work, new learning and new thinking are mandatory for shifting into a mode where people can flourish and thrive. Otherwise, **a rut can quickly turn into a grave for a stubborn company.**

At least once a week I run into a former associate who says, "Man, I don't know what you're into these days, but it's fascinating. I read your articles, but only understand half of it." Some of the new lexicon of innovation can come across as a threat to good-ol'-boy thinking.

The reaction I most often receive is a look of fear, as if I'm a prophet foretelling the end of days. What the articles seek to represent is a generative worldview, one that doesn't settle for the axiomatic logic of "if it ain't broke, don't fix it." From this perspective, **everything in life can be optimized, designed better and carefully crafted to be more relevant.**

A company that will not seek to change their business models, products and services with this sense of restless creativity and forensic exploration of possibility has frozen its growth and fallen into an orthodoxy that will place it on life support and palliative care.

Much like the person who is on the sidelines interested in new ways of thinking but too fearing of learning something new, such companies have stopped encouraging, supporting and rewarding new thinking.

Why? **We should demand that our institutions demand the best of our nature and produce goods and services that enhance and empower life.**

What percentage of people actualize this ideal? How many people long for it, but suppress their calling and compromise the ideal for some rationalized alternative? How many just don't care, and have actually stopped learning, stopped new thoughts and are comfortable in the opiate of a fixed, absolute system?

Look at any example, even the most regulated and formal: the post office, banking or health care. *Nothing stays the same* – and if your company isn't the one welcoming new thinking about your category and making actions to redefine the next iteration of its expression in the market, find the nearest exit.

Ask yourself, when did we stop allowing new thinking?

If you can pinpoint the era when the growth engine was put to rest inside an organization, there is a good chance you can revive it.

No Risk, No Reward:
Innovation Quiz

A good CEO should make the CFO a little nervous. When the CFO is sleeping soundly, the CEO is not reaching high enough and lacks vision.

If the CEO does not provoke people with an aggressive vision of organic growth, someone at the firm needs to be appointed as the official risk-taker. Without risks, there is no reward.

While a company can streamline itself to operational excellence, it still needs to innovate to grow market share. You cannot realize true growth from cost cutting alone.

Innovation requires a different mindset and behaviors than crafting an efficient organization. Businesses need both operational excellence and strategic innovation to prosper in the short- and long-term.

Does your business have a culture that fosters growth and innovation? So many innovation efforts are merely puny attempts to pacify a board request. Worse: when companies believe they are earnest in their innovation efforts, but the culture of the business does not allow for real innovation to happen.

Is your company really innovating or just talking about it?
Take this short quiz by answering "yes" or "no" and find out.

_____People are tasked to plan how to push the boundaries of what seems possible to ensure that we stay ahead.

_____Employees are comfortable asking provocative and unsettling questions about company strategy.

_____Project teams apply offbeat sources in search of the breakthrough solutions.

_____Our organization actively seeks solutions to stay ahead of the curve.

_____Project teams are given time and resources to learn about innovation and trends.

_____We push for continual improvement, even if what we're offering is the industry-leading product or service.

_____Competitors change their offering to mock our business model and market strategy.

_____Failure and smart risk taking are celebrated by our leadership. Efforts do not have to be "successful" to be recognized.

_____There is an active, open culture of dialogue between roles, departments, functions, and levels within the organization.

_____We know that we do not have all the expertise in-house, and partner with firms outside the company to develop new ideas.

_____We purposefully hire people with diverse backgrounds and strive to create teams that are comprised of a variety of disciplines to ensure a wide-sweeping perspective.

_____Good ideas are born from every corner and rank of the company— and there is a formal way to present them and have them seriously considered.

Add up the yeses. Here's the score key.

10-12, rejoice. Your company knows both the wild joys and smart business sense of innovating.

7-9, high five. Your company has a healthy innovation attitude and will be around in the future to celebrate.

4-6, sigh. Well, your company suffers from wanting to innovate but not really understanding how to implement strategic growth across the culture.

0-3, ugh. If you are an employee, you deserve more, hit Monster now. If you own or run the company, it is time to get real. Your competitors will crush you and your best people will leave, soon. Get help, today.

U.S. Corporations are crushing the spirits of their best and brightest

As the resumes roll in for open positions here at the Studio, we are facing a trend we have suspected for a while. There are legions of burned out corporate drones looking for liberation. Study after study shows that Gen X and Gen Y will have more than six jobs in their lifetime, viewing each as a brief stint before their next move.

One report in the *Boston Globe* stated that between 30 and 40 percent of graduates from a selection of top schools, including Harvard and Carnegie-Mellon, are bypassing corporate America and starting their own businesses. Similar reports show that at least half of all Millennials aspire to be self-employed, and view a solo career as more stable than a corporate one.

Young, bright and motivated people are tired of working hard and having their work go nowhere except down the crevices of the corporate bureaucracy. A friend of ours, a brilliant social media and PR strategist just left a global company with Memphis headquarters, exasperated after years of playing politics and waiting for his boss to get promoted or leave so that he could move up a rung. His boss sits in the traffic jam as well, waiting for the Boomers to retire so that he can move up and feel a small sense of accomplishment. Our friend left and has taken a job overseas. Another friend of ours discovered a way to save a cola giant tens of millions of dollars by making a simple policy and financial change. Her suggestion fell on deaf ears; no one wanted to rock the boat. Then a high-level executive heard about the idea and suddenly her group was up for an internal award. Of course they decided to have a more senior colleague represent the team and the idea because he was "funnier."

Bright people are streaming out of corporate America because they want to make an impact. They want to grow businesses. They want have a purpose and make a difference. As it stands today, they are relegated to their cubes. Business is not disrupted when they leave and no one notices they are gone.

Corporate America: you are losing your best people. You are left with the worker bees (a very important part of the team to be sure) and the politicians. These people are mired in old ways of thinking and doing things "the way they have always been done."

The problem is you, not them. They want what all bright people require: intellectual stimulation, autonomy, and entrepreneurial incentives.

Fortune 500: you want to innovate? Empower your younger workforce to think creatively. Give them and their innovative ideas access to top leadership. Break the ladder and shatter the concept of pay grades — promote them over their status quo managers. Shake things up. The days of the rank and file and the gold watch are gone. Your Boomer management will be gone soon too.

Then what?

What's Good for the Bee
is Good for the Hive.

Marcus Aurelius noted that, "If a thing is not *good for the hive*, it is not *good* for the bee." This statement has profound implications for corporate cultures. In a workplace setting, anything that keeps a culture from dynamically regenerating itself is harmful to its people.

If a culture prohibits its people from progressing, pursuing their core passions, and seeing their work reach its potential; it will drive away its high-performance talent. In essence, they will poison the hive and seal the fate for the next phase, or downward spiral, of the enterprise.

Such thinking as "restructuring" or "reorg" may have been in vogue during the Industrial Era, which author Bruce Nussbaum calls the old economy, or the "efficiency economy" in his book *Creative Intelligence*. As we begin to realize that we have optimized our economic engines for total efficiency, cost cutting has only a short-term gain and a severe long-term cost. This real long-term cost may be the pollution of a company culture, the death of a once popular product, or the dilution of market capitalization and brand equity.

To re-energize an organization — its workforce — firms must make the leap from the Efficiency Economy to a Creative Economy. In the Creative Economy, innovation is the key that unlocks value. The thresholds to be crossed on the way to this new orientation of business are based in human factors.

One: you must know the people who use your service or product with sincere empathy. Hang out at their homes. Shadow them at their factories, at work, and during breaks. Take them shopping. Relax with them. Ask about their lives.

Two: you must celebrate and empower your professionals to become creative agents based on what they learn from your customers. This is a very human-to-human equation—and it has the power to re-humanize our places of work

It is a very human urge to make, to create, to invent—harness this natural tendency without a stranglehold of corporate management and death-by-PowerPoint. Create a framework to allow this creative flourishing. This way, your best people stay and the top-line grows in the Creative Economy. As futurist Allen Tolfer wisely predicted, "The illiterate of the 21st century will not be those who cannot learn, read, and write, but those who cannot learn, unlearn, and relearn." Let your bees be bees, and let them act naturally to grow the organization organically. Too much trimming and hive-shaking leaves the business concern with nothing potent enough to self-pollenate its growth.

Real Leadership: Don't Mean a Thing If It Ain't Got That Thing

The American Master of Music, Duke Ellington, also stands as an ideal role model of leadership for the emerging business and nonprofit world. As the global workplace moves toward open workspaces and sees the value of multi-dimensional team filled with hard-to-traditionally-manage creative professionals, a look into Ellington's leadership style can inspire outstanding results.

The master key to Ellington's style was knowing that creativity is a team sport. Collaboration, whether with songwriters or musicians, galvanized a single idea, turning into a massive alchemical expression with more creative power than an individual has to offer. He was always open to exploring works-in-progress with an obsession and passion so rare he named his autobiography *Music Is My Mistress*. He was open to finding what worked to unlock the best product possible, drawing on different musical traditions, different partnerships, and different expressive styles to make the music sound "like a girl saying *yes*," which was his wry way of saying the magic power of collaboration worked.

Another element in Ellington's leadership style was creating a group framework that mixed form (the formal structure of a composition) with areas within that form that allowed for and encouraged, even demanded, improvisation (personal expression within the confines of the project). This mix of structure and creativity within the structure played to the strength of individuals. This point depends on the next one to resonate; he knew his peoples' particular talents deeply.

It is important to note that many of the best players left the Ellington fold, but most eventually returned. Without exception, their reputation, their legacy, and their memories rest on the time spent with Ellington. Something in his nurturing leadership style left them less capable of expressing themselves as fully, as freely away from his influence. He knew his team so well, you could posit, that he was better able to judge what they did best than they were. Ellington showcased his players in miniature masterpieces, displaying a soloist against the backdrop of a tightly knit ensemble. His players knew when to support and when to lead.

Ellington could take variety of backgrounds (formally trained, raw talent, hot shots, team players, the driven, the disciplined) and weave them into a singular force via his vision, strategy, and trust-building style. His music stressed the unique contributions of each band member, fashioned into something greater, into "music that sounds good."

Finally, he let the product — the music — speak for itself. Duke was elegantly dismissive of analysis: "too much talk," he said, "stinks up the place."

Listen to Ellington's music as you would read a book on leadership — his canon is filled with sonic pleasures and profound lessons on organization.

Necessary Disruptions

Last year the *New Yorker* published an article about how Disruptive Innovations have failed and how the theory is bogus. It's one article among a number that, to our thinking, completely underestimates the forward-thinking and world-changing power of disruptive innovation in business.

The long piece went into great depth about the emerging Disruption industry of consultants, the Disruption ethos prevalent in Silicon Valley, and the many Disruption discussions in boardrooms across the globe.

As practitioners of innovation methodologies, we were asked our take on the piece. The writer, Jill Lepore, takes the innovation author, professor, guru, Clayton Christensen, to task. In short, the article is more of an abstruse diatribe on theory, rather than a study of the application of disruptive innovation. Ms. Lepore claims that aiming for disruption is ruining what is left of civilization, that we are creating better gadgets, but not a better planet or better quality of life.

The article is a dense, yet potent read. While she makes some good points with flair rare for academics, the basis of her argument sits on shaky ground. You must understand that disruption — revolutions, not evolutions (think Skype or Netflix as opposed to AT&T buying Direct TV, for example) are needed in more sectors of the world more than ever. But, Ms. Lepore is correct that if the outcome is merely a better gadget, then it may not be worth much outside the bank.

This is the hard part, denial. If you think the world is not in crisis, you may stop reading now. However, we live in an era of change when most of our major systems have shown life-threatening stress. Look at the national debt, climate change, mounting tensions in the Middle East. One glance shows that all of the major systems – the environment, the economy, the educational system, the healthcare system, our coal-based energy system — are in crisis. Only brave, radical solutions can redeem them. Only alternative disruptions can make the types of changes that point a way out of these vexing predicaments. So, even if the methods first birthed a new gadget, then disruptive innovations can now be used to save these systems, the planet, our species, other species—and improve our quality of life. But there is a problem …

The stranglehold that the Industrial Revolution mindset has put on management has created an inflexible, linear choke on innovation. We use methods such as six sigma to wrest results out of a process, which does not allow for incremental (small) innovations to happen organically as part of the oral tradition of a culture. Therefore, businesses and organizations get stuck in a rigid rut and only a revolution can get them unstuck from this over-managed, overly rational way of doing things. We live in an era where our major systems are in crisis—and there is a distrust in human creativity to lead us out of these crises.

When orthodoxies and prejudices will not allow us to dynamically adapt, disruptions are a natural occurrence of a rebirth after a long period of stagnation. Because of the Industrial Era and its paradigm that has been taught in B-school and its shadow over work culture and culture at large, disruptions are the only way to improve the quality of life for the mass of humanity. There are many stories that Ms. Lepore could have quoted about disruptions in healthcare, in lending, in vertical tower farming to explore the positive side of this applied theory, but she was too busy stepping on Dr. Christensen's mistakes to see the overall need for, and proof for the concept of, necessary disruptions in a world where we overly manage things into a state of paralysis.

The Core Pieces
Setting Up the Innovation Process

Four Elements of a Successful Innovation Boot Camp

After working with more than 100 organizations – from leading non-profits to Fortune 500 companies – this hard-earned mantra about innovation has emerged: Concepts and culture are two critical factors necessary for successful innovation.

Culture is the hard part. Like the muscle memory of 2,000-plus people, culture can keep doing what it always does, never implement concepts, or reject them stillborn. Training a culture to embrace innovation takes commitment, courage and a willingness to change.

Nothing sets the stage for cultural change like a company-wide innovation boot camp. Think of it as a three-day immersion into the heart of potential mixed with a deeply collaborative, fast-paced reorientation of working together.

The only goal is to inspire new, organic growth for an organization. Changing the culture to receive new growth is the prime mover, as culture is made of people primarily.

Naming Ceremony: As the philosopher Alan Watts was keen on saying, "You have to go out of your mind to come to your senses." To establish this mindset, the first exercise is a renaming ceremony.

Therefore, no one at the organization goes through the crucible of the boot camp assuming their self-limited idea of themselves, in their day-to-day role.

This exercise also helps mitigate anyone pulling rank during the process. Later, at a specified time, we have everyone rename themselves their given names, titles, but with an empowering addition; they say "and innovator" after giving their title.

More than good theater, this method works as an effective way to encourage real creativity and collaboration and the beneficial ramifications take permanent hold as the groups handle ongoing project work.

Unrelated Innovation Exercise: Now, it is time to engender creative confidence to a group of people from a variety of departments, including finance, engineering, marketing and sales.

We give them this assurance by having them partner in twos and then complete a 90-minute design thinking exercise.

This microcosm of a complete process gives them the grounding to complete the more challenging project cycle over the two following days. We use an exercise that has nothing to do with business, so they can stay focused on the process itself and not slip into work identities.

Blowing Up the Business Model: With a sly wink, we return to the organization's business model, but with an exploration of how else it can make money.

This Revenue Model exercise is always a revelation to participants. The boon here is that boot campers understand that their business model is not sacrosanct, nor is it reality itself. Rather, it is just a snapshot of their business today, one mental model of a much greater reality rife with possibility.

Identifying Orthodoxies: To end the first day, we like to hold up a mirror about organizational orthodoxies. Giving permission to explore the self-imposed limitations an organization has put on itself unknowingly allows for healthy adaptation, the rebirth of a culture of possibility.

Day one focuses on culture, while days two and three focus on concepts while rewarding the renewed mindset of new growth.

Three Critical Ingredients
for Innovation

Our firm, the Southern Growth Studio, helps many companies with innovation. We help with projects labeled as innovation and we also consult on how companies set up the processes, framework, and governance for successful innovation.

Based on our experience, we know that three key things must be in place for innovation to flourish. If innovation is to become the No. 1 strategy priority to drive growth and wealth creation, these three ingredients must be in place.

First, senior management commitment. Innovation must be in the company's vision, goals, and metrics — and conversations must take place about innovations on a continuous basis. Innovation needs to be valued and practiced as a core disciple of the firm. Senior leaders need to model this importance. Senior management commitment is more than twice as important as any other factor in determining the success of innovation at a company.

Second, teams over technology. Innovation isn't about the collaboration software. It's about people. Multi-disciplinary teams who follow a process with an open spirit of collaboration score best.

Third, define types of innovation. Incremental innovations are wholly different animals compared to breakthrough, game-changing innovations. Define the objective of each project or mission with care so you can better manage expectations.

With these three ingredients in place, a company can use innovation to fuel organic growth.

Entrepreneurs,
Create Your Own Maps.

Entrepreneurialism is the last frontier—an uncharted region with unprecedented, unforeseen, and unknown dangers, challenges, and rewards. All adventures begin with a new map, just like the territory you charted in your business plans. You drafted this plan in the ardor of a visionary impulse, tempered with a will to thrive as you grow.

The world is in too short a supply of courage and craves its heroes, its success stories. Perhaps your story will become a light in our constellation of capitalism, a story that inspires generations, like the ones of Bill Gates, Steve Jobs, or Fred Smith of FedEx.

For the real, budding businessperson, there is no choice. You know you can do something better, create a more useful product or service. The status quo won't cut it. You're propelled to create a better way by aptitude, circumstance, drive, or a combination of all three. Here's the real reason why.

In this new world, you learn who you are, what you're worth, your capacity, who you can trust, and you come to realize – with earned depth and from experience – what things really mean. You can invent your future.

Invent: You must possess a mindset that allows quantum leaps. This is the taproot of the creative process. To invent requires skill, knowledge, and passion. You must be able to lose sense of time when solving a problem while also having the ability to zoom in and zoom out. You zoom into the smallest details of an invention-in-process and then zoom out to see its broadest potential market application, keeping one eye on the product and the other on the market. You adapt, as the actual finish line is not yet on the map.

You: The key word here is you. The tense is possessive. You possess a sense of mission, a calling. You do not sacrifice your integrity for the illusion of security. You take risks because you believe in what you are doing. As a result, you trust yourself and others are willing to bet on you. You leave the safety of tenure or the golden handcuffs of a corporate job to own your personal destiny. You don't have a back-up plan.

Future: The future is the frontier you have begun to map out. Often a new map—a new way of seeing—is placed over an old map and a new era is born. The keys to this future are always found right at hand, in the present moment. Your future is defined by the actions you take today.

Now, a story about a fellow adventurer, a personal star in my constellation, my maternal grandfather, Leo Brody. He had to turn down a full scholarship to Vanderbilt to support his mother and two sisters. While working at a pawnshop on Beale Street he started repairing luggage. Along the way, he dismantled pieces, put them back together better than before, and an idea struck him like lightning. Travel was the new paradigm. Planes, trains, and automobiles had replaced boats and more travelers were on the roads.

He hustled his way to Chicago and New York with his map in hand. He sold all the large department stores on private label luggage. During the heyday of his company, it produced 2.4 million pieces of luggage weekly. At his funeral it was stated that he was one of the rare individuals possessed with a vision and the will to manifest it. In other words, he invented his future.

Now, it's your turn. Such a life is not for the lily livered or faint of heart, but the treasures are varied and worth the effort. Take the step. Follow your calling. The world needs you. Besides, you cannot deny the adventure for another second.

Corporate Shamanism

Take risks. Leap into unknown and unexplored areas. Express yourself in new ways. Do these things to locate, validate, and capitalize on new areas of growth for your business.

There are formal methods and processes for unlocking potential and manifesting new realities. We always tell clients to be true to themselves, their organizations, and to be a positive force on the planet. We embolden and encourage. We connect them to the real lives that use their creations.

For these reasons, we would like to state that real innovation work is a form of Corporate Shamanism.

"Shaman" is a word of the Tungis people of Siberia, which means "one who sees in the dark."

This visionary work dates as far back as 40,000 years ago. A shaman uses the power, wisdom, and energies of a different frame of mind to create and promote constructive change in people and their environments.

A good shaman sees him or herself as a "hollow bone" through which healing and messages are transmitted to clients. Isn't this the same work as an Innovation Catalyst who strives to connect their clients with their own humanity and the humans who use their products and services? Without imposing a pre-amped set of prejudices, innovation starts in the dark of discerning how people perceive your offering.

Then, through a set of rigorous exercises, the energies are harnessed and the perceptions that are gathered are put into a new pattern, a new way of seeing, a new way of measuring value. This creative process holds true on individual, product, and corporate levels.

As organizations are nothing more than collections of individuals, it makes deep sense that these time-tested, powerful methods can be used to restore organizations to a sense of mission, purpose, and optimal creativity. In fact, many actual shamanic practices can be applied to business issues and corporate cultures with great effect.

Besides, Innovation, as a word, has no real meaning anymore. For some organizations it is a lofty goal, for others a marketing plan, and still for others a new IT platform. Yet, real innovations – categorized as Disruptive or Breakthrough – change the world they inherited.

While it seems like a wild leap of fancy, calling the discipline Corporate Shamanism instead of that empty word "innovation" from the Industrial Revolution, is a better fit.

Corporate Shamanism re-humanizes business, focuses on the people who use a product or services, and uses a scientific approach to achieving a visionary result.

Who wants to journey into the vast land of possibility? Let's go.

No Time for Chickens

As we meet with more and more of the midmarket companies in America, we are astounded at how many of them are hiding under their desk "riding the recession out."

The old "Story of Chicken Little" comes to mind: Chicken Little was in the woods one day when an acorn fell on her head. It scared her so much that she trembled all over. She shook so hard, half her feathers fell out. Chicken Little is a story for teaching courage and it seems that courage is what the midmarket lacks. This is troubling given that the midmarket is the backbone of the American economy.

The National Center for the Middle Market at Ohio State University's Fischer College of Business conducts the largest survey of the midmarket. The survey of nearly 1,500 midmarket C-level executives concludes: "the health of the middle market is vital to overall U.S. prosperity." The center estimates that the midmarket encompasses 195,000 businesses and contributes 34 percent of total employment in the US. The study categorized only nine percent of the midmarket companies as "growth champions" that exhibited double-digit revenue growth in 2010 and 2011, and projected the same for the rest of 2012.

According to Doug Farren, Director of the National Center for the Middle Market, the characteristics that set growth champions apart from slower-growing companies include: having a sharper focus on customers, investing in innovation, having a broader geographic vision for their business, cultivating a strong management culture, and doing a superior job with talent management. "It's not who you are, it's what you do that makes you a growth champion," said Farren.

Investment in innovation was the strongest common theme across growth champions, he said. They tend to invest 2.5 times more into R&D per sales dollar than slower-growing companies.

Midmarket company executives that want to ascend the ladder from marginal growth into growth champions should ask themselves some key questions, including whether they allocate and protect funding for innovation, and how they can strengthen innovation and make it repeatable and measurable.

The recession is a time of opportunity for smart companies to out-maneuver the competitive field and for strong companies to put capital to work. It is the perfect landscape to enact strategy and make strides in the market.

Here at the Studio we frequently discuss the paralysis that occurs in the face of change and the desire to take calculated risk but the inability to pull the trigger: all part of the human condition. Our working theory at the moment is that growth and innovation isn't possible without growth in the team and in the individual. To us, growth means expansion of the mind to empower humankind to walk through and explore the unknown in the fabled "door number two."

The midmarket needs a shot in the arm. Don't be a Chicken Little. Don't be afraid. No, that's not the sky falling. In fact, it may be opportunity knocking.

The Right ROI
of Innovation for Your Firm

Innovation as investment is a simple three-step process. First, figure out the risk-tolerance level, which allows you to get real with your expectations, roles, resources, and metrics. Second, come up with a mix based on the risk-tolerance level of your culture. Third, formalize the assignment – and kick off all projects with visible executive leadership support. This executive support is critically important.

Let's demonstrate in broad strokes. You and a core team are assigned to make innovation real at XYZ firm, a mid-market manufacturing and product company in the B2B space. Traditionally, XYZ firm has been risk-averse and managed with rigorous metrics. After one failed trial innovation project almost a decade ago, the leadership felt burned and buckled down to achieve operational excellence. Now, growth seems possible – more growth than five or seven percent a year. Also, the board has been inquiring more insistently about innovation and wants XYZ to reach double-digits growth and to explore innovation.

So, we know that XYZ firm has a low risk-tolerance. Therefore, they can develop an innovation mix that works for their firm. XYZ decides on an 80/15/5 strategy. Eighty percent of its innovation efforts will be incremental to their existing operating business and will include product augmentations, new products in existing lines, and some process optimization (cost savings) not yet realized. Incremental innovation requires the least amount of change and spending but traditionally brings the smallest returns. New metrics and a few committees are created for existing product managers, engineers, marketing and R&D, and a small budget is set aside.

Fifteen percent is focused on bringing something new to the firm. We will classify this as a Disruptive Innovation. The firm reassigns a product manager as an innovation manager, allocates a small percentage of a multi-disciplinary team to this 15 percent effort and creates metrics for new ideas. They will follow a stage-gate process and will be allowed to present new ideas for product suites and services four times a year to senior leadership. For a roughly 250K total investment, they estimate a return of 1.2 million to 2 million in 18-24 months.

The remaining 5 percent is a conservative bet on a breakthrough innovation, something that will possibly redefine how the market thinks about a category while making the company that creates the breakthrough the market leader in the space. XYZ firm needs to not reject the ideas that come from this assigned 5 percent of the innovation ROI as outlandish or too wild as a matter of planning – it is their job to foresee trends and craft stunning ways to meet unmet needs for their customers. Therefore, they establish in their founding metrics that they will pilot at least one of these ideas within an 18-month period as part of a formal study.

Innovation ultimately is an investment. You must diversify and apply a mix that is right for your firm to make it a formal discipline.

Growth: That Crazy Talk

Call it the entrepreneurial instinct, innovation, business savvy, whatever you want: strategic growth is how business prospers.

While iconic ventures stand as global luminaries of category-defining growth, such as the modern grocery store and overnight delivery, most businesses cower when facing growth.

Growth is a natural source of power, a wellspring or volcano. Businesses, like nature, live a lifecycle. Organizations are as alive as a person; yet, most businesses do not harness the growth process to gain an advantage. Rare companies that address growth by a mix of planning and making well-timed, well-orchestrated adaptions to their plan make positive headlines.

In most cases, dynamics change market conditions and businesses retrench. They do more of what no longer works with increased vigor and focus. They react in fear. These actions dig a grave.

More than ever, every business needs to find, discover, and implement fresh, rewarding ways to procure and retain business. Remain relevant, demonstrate value, and compete with formally unthinkably high levels of service.

At the time when companies need to radically rethink their market strategy, they hide behind walls of denial and the sleepy, sentimental practices that worked in the 70s, 80s or 90s.

Sadly, we witness this reenactment at business after business: "Growth. What do you mean? We're just sitting, waiting for the phone to ring. ... We don't need a plan. ... We just trade customers back and forth with our competition," and on and on. We get thrown out for *crazy talk*.

Excuses and justifications, we've heard them all. They add up to a deafening wake up call for the whole business culture of Planet Earth.

Consider your business. Do you really want to become one of hundreds of companies that were industry leaders in the cultural climate that once was? An example of the perfect company for its era, long ago? Or, can we retool our business climate and invent new product pipelines and services that create new markets and generate serious returns?

What will this generation's visionaries look like? What core markets will they disrupt or create? How will they impact the world and infuse the local economy by being a top employer and recruiter for the area? Perhaps it will grow out of your neighborhood?

Let's apply this crazy talk to existing companies. What old-line companies will transform their business model and product/service mix to keep growing? What companies will quicken their demise by not changing? These are crazy times. Listen to the crazy talk.

Here's what keeps you sane: accept the fact that growth is a reality in business. What keeps you inspired is seeing your topline revenue grow because you guided change in your favor. You have a strategy. You adapt. You keep the firm in the present moment, instead of living a tired dream and repeating outmoded practices.

Will the next company be ready to grow, stand up? The world needs you.

Front End Innovation

Business Becomes Human

An R&D scientist once said to me, "We need to always begin new product development projects this way," after sifting through more than 20 in-depth consumer narratives of their condition. These people went into great details about their lives, their struggles, their rituals, and their beliefs. As we unpacked their learnings, the scientist understood the complexities of having a rich, full contextual understanding of the people for whom he will design new, innovative solutions. To summarize with a metaphor, he walks in their high heels, sneakers, and Crocks, embodying their situation as if it were his own.

Instead of creating another product barely distinguishable from the sea of sameness that surfeits the shelves of food, drug, and mass stores off of a job brief that solves a marketing line problem, this scientist can now collaborate on a new approach to these problems with a deep understanding of the situation.

The insight at hand is that we are not solving business problems here. We are solving human problems. In this era when landfills and the seas are gutted with enough plastic to choke the planet, do we really need another product for the sake of making money solely? Wouldn't it be better if we create things people need, people use, and that help people? Please do not tell me that this is idealistic.

This is the business-world paradigm shift of our era. Forget business-to-business. Forget business-to-consumer. That is outdated thinking.
We are crafting solutions for real people. Instead of creating a me-too product for an ambiguous market segment, real innovations seek to connect with the fate and fabric of their users' lives. This is human-to-human business and smart product design, part caused-based and part entrepreneurial horse sense, but it makes business good and it also, no surprise, makes good business.

Following this human-centric process, Design Thinking, begins with empathy with real people. Later, product ideas are co-created with real people. This hand-on-the-pulse method creates new, breakthrough products and services that make a positive difference in the lives of many.

Are You an Empathetic Professional?

As a professional, as a leader, even as a brand, ask yourself this critical question: are you empathetic? Do you have the genuine ability to "understand and share the feelings of another?"

More research is showing us the power of empathy, as it can be used as the tissue that connects and deepens relationships. With empathy, you walk in the other's high heels or sneakers, feel their feelings, experience life from their perspective. Human brains are filled with mirror neurons, which not only react to our subjects of empathy, but also reproduce their emotions.

However, there is a dark side of pure empathy, called pain. Ongoing neuroscientific research tells us that when we feel the stress of others, we take on their pain.

"Empathy is really important for understanding others' emotions very deeply, but there is a downside of empathy when it comes to the suffering of others," says Olga Klimecki, a researcher at the Max Planck Institute for Human Cognitive and Brain Sciences in Germany. "When we share the suffering of others too much, our negative emotions increase. It carries the danger of an emotional burnout."

Whereas the first question is, are you empathetic? The second one is, are you compassionate? A recent study, published in the journal Cerebral Cortex, suggests that we can better cope with others' negative emotions by strengthening our own skills for compassion, which the researchers define as "feeling concern for another's suffering and desiring to enhance that individual's welfare."

Training in compassion allowed participants who are empathetic to better cope with despair. With more and more evidence, we see that empathy is a gateway into the others' experiences, but compassion is the arch through which you want to do something to help the other without robbing them of any wise life lessons.

While there is a lot of press about the power of empathy, it only takes you half the way to the point of creativity, of wanting to craft a solution that fits the situation. In pure empathy, due to neuroplasticity, you can get lost in the emotions of others.

Compassion, defined as "sympathetic pity and concern for the sufferings or misfortunes of others," means that you care enough to try and help. Compassion also mitigates against the negativity, allowing our brains to respond in a grounded, positive manner to tough news or hard feedback.

This is great news if you plan on creating or improving a product or service or being a good leader of people, as you can tap this deep reservoir of humanity to create something of value, something useful, and something that fills an unmet need or sets something crooked straight. Likewise, if you are in a management position you can earn trust by being empathetic with your employees.

Empathy creates the bridge, and compassion points out a new path. This new path is what meaningful innovation seeks to be in the market.

Business Anthropology

Many consumer product, retail, and software companies are reinventing themselves and growing market share by better empathizing with the people who use their products or services. Increasingly, other businesses—from B2B companies to doctor clinics—are learning the potent power of empathy.

Traditional market research and connection tools only take insight so far. To build a real bridge for innovation and new product efforts, new applications and approaches were needed to supplement the old mix.

While some aspects of this trend are labeled as Design Thinking or User Experience, the field gives rise to a new role: anthropologist or ethnographer. Whether it is a retail, consumer, or business anthropologist, these specialists take an immersive approach to getting to know the people for whom products and services are being created.

Companies such as Proctor & Gamble, Target, and the Mayo Clinic have gained insights that create new markets using this method. Empathy is the key here. Business anthropology unlocks the opportunities.

Disclosure: Because this discipline is so rare in our part of the U.S., I interviewed an employee of our company about this growing trend and her role as anthropologist/ethnographer, Cole Bradley.

What is ethnography?

Strictly speaking, ethnography is a qualitative research method used to understand a population through empirical evidence.

How is ethnography a useful tool for businesses?

For businesses, understanding the lives, desires, motivations, and habits of their client is critical for providing the right products and services to the right people. This is where ethnography is crucial. You can make assumptions about a person's purchasing habits or service needs, or you can discover what's beyond their wallet through direct interaction and communication. This discovery process is the cornerstone of ethnography.

How can ethnographic methods be applied to business?

Where business can truly benefit from ethnography is through consistent and systematic application of techniques. The models can also be applied within the business. Want to reduce turnover, increase worker satisfaction, or streamline a process? Don't assume a top-down approach. Oftentimes, the person with the most insight is the person actually doing the job, and ethnographic exercises are ideal for vetting the expert knowledge and experiences of your team.

Why is a human-centered way of doing business more important than ever?

In a mass produced society, we are desperate to know that our individuality and sense of self are being cared for through the things we purchase, be it an iPod or a yoga class. People want to feel that the product or service they are buying is right for them as a unique entity. Ethnography can be vital to determining what drives a specific group or individual so that their experience feels more personal and fulfills that need for connection.

What is the most surprising thing you have discovered working in the private sector?

How much a person's network influences who they are and what they do. Even though we are increasingly disconnected- from our food, our people, our heritage, our planet- we still seek the advice of those closest to us, just like we have done for the last 200,000 years. From where to get a haircut to what type of job we should do to who we should marry, we rely on other people to guide us. We like to think we are secluded in our decision making, that we're islands of choices, but it's simply not true. We need our networks.

Design Thinking:
A Tested Method for
Creating Breakthrough Innovation

While the word "innovation" thunders from the boardroom and from the ranks, few companies actually build a sustainable process for generating real solutions that create value. Instead, they hastily focus on un-validated and over-caffeinated pet ideas of the CEO. Or worse, they spend a lot of time and resources recreating a slightly different version of their same core offering.

The two, too common scenarios noted above are not innovation. Real innovation is not a product line extension or an additional feature. Spare us. The world is already surfeited with such nonsense.

Real innovation requires thinking outside of your own business paradigm.

Real innovations that make major traction in the market solve problems people didn't know they had. Real innovations get out of the office and embody the matter. They walk in the shoes of the intended audience, even visit them at home or their office. They begin with *empathy,* then follow an iterative process, and then reap substantial rewards.

This formal innovation process was named just a few years ago. While it remains contested, Design Thinking is a set of principles—from mindset and roles to process—that work for consumer products, software, services, even in the social sector.

Design Thinking is a method for solving complex problems. Think of Design Thinking as installing a new operating system for life: it's that revolutionary. Looking at the world with an inspired eye for redesigning every aspect that could be improved is the mindset. There are few experiences that could not be improved.

As noted by Tim Brown, now the CEO of IDEO, there are three spaces to explore, which overlap: inspiration, ideation, and implementation. Here's the skinny version:

Inspiration: the problem or opportunity that motivates the search for solutions: this stage involves interviewing, observing, sketches, mock-ups, and scenario-building.

Ideation: the process of generating, developing, and testing ideas: this stage involves building prototypes & exploring the balance between practical functionality and emotional appeal.

Implementation: the path that leads from the project room to the market: this stage involves clearly communicating the idea and proving/showing that it will work, and validating a business model for the concept.

Design Thinking follows a seven-step framework: *define, research, ideate, prototype, choose, implement,* and *learn.* These steps overlap one another and are repeated in iterations to produce concepts that work.

While Design Thinking came out of product development, graphic design, and engineering fields, its processes and spaces are being adopted by research and development, marketing, and product management departments in many firms across the globe.

The process requires some non-linear thinking and allows for the devil's advocate role to be voiced. For these reasons, many companies cannot allow it into their culture—to their own detriment and decline.

Companies such as Proctor & Gamble, Target, Apple, IKEA, as well as Bank of America, the Mayo Clinic and a host of others you know by name are defining market trends and market cap by employing elements of Design Thinking in their innovation efforts.

If your boardroom and hallways thunder with the call to innovate, get real. Try some processes with proven efficacy. Don't just rush into tomorrow the same as yesterday with a little more haste and stress.

The Hardest Part.

For many in the innovation field, the hardest task is listening—real listening, deep listening. To listen without building a mental model or rushing to a conclusion is a cultivated skill. To listen to a person's summary of your product or service and honor their experience as the only experience that matters is not only a great courtesy, but it can be a competitive advantage; that is, if you are willing to collect feedback from a lot of customers and apply adaptive intelligence.

The hardest part is just listening.

In the Design Thinking methodology of innovation, the first major phase is empathy. Empathy is defined by Merriam-Webster as "the feeling that you understand and share another person's experiences and emotions: the ability to share someone else's feelings." Really feeling the feelings of your customers means walking in their high heels or loafers. What it really means is surrendering all of your pre-set and pre-amp notions of what you may mean to them and approaching the session with a receptive, open ear. As our Buddhist friends say, you must see their experience with a Beginner's Mind.

Once they start pointing out where they get confused or frustrated, the hardest part is just listening. Your hands starts shaking when taking notes. You may catch yourself wanting to instruct them on "proper" usage of your product or service, but then you remember, it's their experience and they are the customer. You are just here to collect information. There will be a time for clustering for trends and developing theories. There will be a time to make revisions and test them. Right now, in this moment of empathy collecting, your role is to listen deeply—and that's a metaphoric mountain you have to climb, the hard part, just listening.

Only after you have paid respects to those you serve by listening and collecting enough empathies sans personal or corporate bias can you begin to reframe or define the next steps. At this point in the empathy phase listening to the patterns and trends that emerge is the hardest part.

What you find may unlock many fresh perspectives, ideas for sustainable competitive advantage, and new ways to take care of unmet customer needs. But you need to listen and that's the hard part.

Primary Research.
Personal Legends.
Talking Sticks.

Businesses, organizations, and non-profits grow with the level of first-hand experiences they have with their prospects, customers, members, or donors. These entities both know themselves and also know their audience, their tribe.

This is the Relationship Age – the era of paying attention. Think of it as winning business by paying respect.

To know yourself you have to go through a detailed strategic process and carefully, consciously create a vibrant culture. To know your audience, you have to learn to respect people deeply. The primacy of compassionate and sensitive primary, first-hand, narrative research is the key that unlocks this world of possibilities.

The hardest thing for organizations to do to accomplish such growth is to realize that traditional marketing research and segmentation is outmoded. The reason: it looks at the people with whom it should be trying to cultivate a relationship as a target, a one-dimensional object, rather than a fully alive human subject with a treasure trove of stories, memories, dreams, hopes, and fears. In summary, the old method edits out the humanity. And, winning the innovation game is about touching humanity, creating something of value for real people.

When the author of *The Alchemist* and other books, Paulo Coelho, was inducted into the Brazilian Academy of Letters, he said, "The glory of the world is transitory, and we should not measure our lives by it, but by the choice we make to follow our personal legend, to believe in our utopias, and to fight for our dreams." And then he wrote, "We are all protagonists of our own lives, and it is often the anonymous heroes who make the deepest mark."

By honoring people in this spirit, primary research gets to the heart of the matter—the human experience with a product, service, or organization—and taps into the personal legends of each of the people with whom they are working.

Many of the people working in this field are consumer anthropologists who have been trained to listen respectfully, probe deeply, and stay attuned for verbal and non-verbal clues. This tradition goes back to pre-history days in the legend of the Taking Stick. The Talking Stick was a method used by Native Americans, to let everyone speak their mind during a council meeting, a type of tribal meeting. According to the indigenous Americans' tradition, the stick was imbued with spiritual qualities that called up the spirit of their ancestors to guide them in making good decisions. The stick ensured that all members who wished to speak had their ideas heard. All members of the circle were valued equally.

The rules of the Talking Stick follow: Whoever holds the talking stick has within their hands the power of words. Only they can speak while holding the stick, and the other council members must remain silent. The eagle feather tied to the stick gives the speaker the courage and wisdom to speak truthfully and wisely. The rabbit fur on the end of the stick reminds him that his words must come from his heart.

The history of AA (Alcoholic Anonymous) and other step programs and the practice of psychotherapy are all based on this awareness: that speaking the truth is healing. But it is healing for the group as a whole because as each individual listens, in silence and reverence, a whole world of understanding opens up.

This world of understanding becomes the basis of innovations that make lives better and makes organizations more meaningful and significant.

Go Deep or Go Home
in the Era of Innovation

We meet companies and non-profits who have been marketing to the same lists for years. Often, these lists and the assumptions about the people on their lists are more than a decade old. These aged lists may have been scrubbed, but that is simply for those who have fallen off the grid, one way or another. This point should be obvious to any reader of this book: there are major problems with this scenario.

First off, organizations marketing to the same list for years lose the feel of how their buyers make decisions. Their selling instincts dull, and then they tend to think of names on the list as objects rather than subjects with rich, full lives, motivations, and choices. In essence, they lose their hunting impulse, their sense of courtship, and reduce a potentially valuable customer relationship into a vague, impersonal slot machine, settling for a single trans-action with low odds.

Second, people are dynamic, not static. If these organizations put their prospects into a rigid category instead of knowing them on a deeper level, they will be marketing to a snapshot that is no longer valid. Think of yourself or your children 10 years ago to demonstrate this point. People are one of the most progressive species on the planet. Fortunes can be made, lost, and regained in a decade—and if your customer information keeps the same basic inputs, you are out of touch with reality.

Third, your weakest competitors are marketing to the exact same list. Incredibly, they are marketing to them with a similar value proposition, brand promise, feature and benefit set, and price range (perhaps with a few incremental differences, but nothing really discernible to them). They, too, are eking out a living on the after-fumes of cobwebbed insights from a decade ago, and cannot think outside of the confines of a strategy set when the world was a different place.

Fourth, the most egregious sin: They don't have any actionable insights about the market, the people in the market, the trends and forces that shape the market, and they do not renew and transform their innovation and marketing efforts to position as a leader in their category. This is the classic deadly sin of sloth. If it exists in your organization, eradicate it or risk extinction.

Face it: this is the post-industrial world, the economic era of innovation. These innovations are steeped in human-to-human valves—offering products, services, causes, and messages that add value to a person's life. You have to know a person to go this deep. You must immerse yourself in their world and get out of your conference room to comprehend where and how you can really add value.

Call it a deep dive, a voice of the customer, an ethnography, narrative insight based marketing research, field studies, whatever—just get out of your own head and your rut-like routines and get inside the homes, routines, rituals, and hearts of your people. Honor those that buy from you or give to you, as subjects with dynamic lives.

By investing in them, you create a win-win relationship. You offer something of value to Joe, Betty, John, Veena, and Amir—and they, in return, return to your offering as part of the natural course of their lives. This quid pro quo, these repeat sales, will not happen if you keep playing the old lists game and never spend time with your prospect base. Go deep.

Trendcasting and Innovation

Did you wake up this morning to realize that the world has changed and your business has not changed with it? Many companies of all sizes are dying a slow death in a saturated market with outdated business models. They fail to get out ahead of what's next.

Business leaders commonly attribute growth issues to a stagnant market or corporate dependency on an inferior product. These are excuses – the heart of the issue is a short-term and reactive corporate mindset. The antidote is to install a culture of proactive forethought to replace the more typical reactive market strategies.

We encourage our clients to take up trendcasting – the practice of tracking and forecasting global trends that will affect their business. This relatively new term has been used mostly for tracking and predicting consumer behavior, but we believe that it is also useful for studying industries and a productive innovation tool for those seeking growth and transformation.

To do this, you should task a group of employees with professionally diverse backgrounds to become a band of trend-spotters and form a think tank of sorts within the company. The team's objective is to uncover emerging trends that are three to five years out. To start, they have to take a snapshot of where things are today so that they have defined a baseline for future trends. Done right, this is not just a research effort to read analyst reports and round up their assessment of existing trends. The idea is to see what others do not and to predict the next wave of trends. Have the team investigate the macroeconomic factors at work in both the global economy and the industry. They should also study the regulations underway and those that might come down the pike. Once they have a handle on current established trends, they can begin to evaluate all of the possible impacts that might set off new trends.

At this point, it may be helpful to bring in a third party to facilitate the discussion and prompt the team to stretch their thinking. Industry experience and basic human cognitive bias will cloud their ability to see beyond what happened in the past and project into a new and unexpected future.

Be on the lookout for fads, a pet rock-like flash in the pan. It is important to define a set of indicators and parameters to evaluate the size, impact, and likelihood of the trend materializing. This will give the team a framework to assess risk and determine if the prospective trend is just an element to be factored in to the strategy or whether it is significant enough to warrant an innovation effort.

Unfortunately, there is no magic formula that validates trends with 100 percent certainty. However, quantitative models that assess probability and risk are useful tools when considering investment. Pinpointing emerging trends is critical to defining the boundaries for a successful innovation effort. If you want to grow through innovation, you must first understand existing trends and then trendcast to discover what might be next.

Use Your Senses.

Design Thinking serves as a valuable tool for defining problems, exploring core empathy with customers, and discovering new, surprising, and game-changing innovations in products, services, and experiences.

However, Design Thinking has its limits, the core shortcoming being that it uses only one of the five senses and other ways of knowing as the primary mode of creation. Because Design Thinking came out of the design and engineering world, the solutions tend to be visual.

There are more modes of creation and knowing, which allow different styles of thinkers to fully participate in innovation projects. The world of innovation needs to widen its dominant modes of discovery to include inventions that present themselves in ways other than visual.

The various forms of clairvoyance provide new methods of ideation and conceptual thinking. We recommend exploring at the idea generating stage first with each mode. You never know what mode may crack the code of growth and provide real value to your business.

Keep in mind that, in the ideation phase, a basic download has already occurred and we seek new ideas, which is more of an art than a science. Later in the process, we apply the critical facilities in the Validation phase of the project.

Here is a short list of some of the non-visual sensory modes:

Feeling/Touching: Clairsentience. Here, a person acquires insight primarily by feeling. Kinesthetic learners thrive when they can feel an idea or touch a concept, making creation a "hands-on" experience. Actually doing an activity can be the easiest way for them to learn. Mapping out an experience, as in asking "how does it feel when … ?", can make the feeling mode valuable and immediate. After all, innovations make tired categories easier to use and create a better experience. Sometimes, the way the category should feel arises in these sessions – and serves as a tuning fork for the entire project lifecycle.

Hearing/Listening: Clairaudience. In this mode, insights form first as a sound – sometimes a whole word and sometimes a hum or a syllable – and people who excel in this style discern deeply, listening with a "third ear" attuned to auditory impressions. We recommend a Deep Listening session – where we seek to define the tone and pitch of the category of the innovation. Many ideas spring out from these "seed syllables."

Smelling: Clairalience. The olfactory senses have long been called the gateway of the soul. How should a product or place smell – and how do you map out the associations that arise in the process. How does a poorly performing category smell now, whether it's a store, a doctor's office, or a restaurant. Smart companies, like Westin Hotels, know the value of defining a particular scent.

Knowing: Claircognizance. The hunch. Sometimes you know something from the gut. This form of knowledge is an intuitive download. Many business people, artists, and scientists have written about intuition. After an immersion into a problem, practice ways to tap the intuition of the team members. Acknowledge the knowing as it presents itself to group members in a way that is non-judgmental. As Dr. Norman Sheely says, "Every invention is an intuitive download." Einstein agrees: "The intuitive mind is a sacred gift."

Tasting: Clairgustance. In this mode, you turn on your taste buds – and taste a substance without putting anything in your mouth. Popular culture has a keen expression: "That left a bad taste in my mouth." Woe be on the company that leaves a bad taste in a customer's mouth. How should an experience taste? That is the question.

Design Thinking works for visual thinkers, but it is a big world with a complex range of senses. All of these senses can be harnessed to create breakthrough innovations.

Defining Which Problem to Solve

Innovation Risks Bring Rewards

Suppose we told you that you could spend $185,000 and turn it into $25 million or more in a few years. You would accuse us of phishing, an investment scam, or dismiss the proposition as foolhardy. Yet, these are the types of returns we see from clients and those in the world who invest in breakthrough innovation at their companies.

Whether it is a product firm, a service organization, or a business-to-business company, these types of return on investment take on nominal risk and garner a large reward. This risk: an unblinking willingness to do something outside of your current operating and business models, and a small amount of capital and talent.

To explore, take one half of an internal resource and tell them to choose an innovation firm for a vexing challenge the organization has not been able to solve to date. The innovation firm will cost between an estimated $75,000 and $125,000 for the entire challenge. Then, recruit a variety of internal people to serve on the project team, giving them about 20 to 25 percent of their time and a small travel budget, if needed.

Design an eight-to-12-week innovation sprint. During the first week, the devoted internal resource and the innovation firm will create a project plan, kick off the project team, and immerse themselves in the value-creating journey.

The first step is to design the challenge carefully – the devoted half resource and Innovation Firm can handle this task. Then, take the project team into the field to actually talk with those for whom they will design a solution. Call this the Empathy phase. This deep qualitative work, done by a mix of roles (managers, sales, RnD, IT, etc.) helps in several, key ways: breaking the deadlock of rushing to product development with someone's pet idea and also understanding how the organization's creations impact the real lives of people. This is human-to-human business. After many interviews are collected, the team debriefs the interviews and develops themes.

Next, the problem is defined.

A portfolio of ideas will be generated, vetted, refined, and tested again. In this process, the testing cycles cost less than large batches of quantitative modeling, and are typically more on target. After a portfolio of concepts has been through this cycle three or four times, you can spend the remaining time writing a business case.

From Swiffer to the Spin toothbrush to the Dirt Devil to children's CT scanning devices to better treatment at the Cleveland Clinic, this radical investment story is similar. But it comes with a warning.

If you are not allocating a tiny portion of your overall spending on innovation, your competition probably is. With their additional $25 million, they will be able to buy you at the fire sale.

Foresight is Better than Insight.

Given advances in market research, innovation methods, and data analysis, insights should aim for being less descriptive and more predictive.
The highest and best value of business is to find new opportunities and plug into emerging trends, rather than make deeper sense of what already exists. These envisioning roles and departments should be renamed the Foresight department rather than Insight.

Insight is valuable, no doubt, but in our era of data dashboards and operational excellence, any analyst can provide a snapshot of revenue, market penetration, inventory, performance, project progress with the click of a mouse. Even slight forecasting, such as revenue projections with a known product or service, can be handled as a basic descriptive budgeting exercise. Giving a description of *what is* is simply a matter of good business practice today. Insightful, but nothing special.

What really levers growth is being able to discern unmet needs in the market and shape shifting the business model and operations of an organization enough to welcome a burgeoning opportunity.

If business really exists to bring value to its shareholders and customers, then it has a moral imperative that they do two things at the same time.

One: Attain operational excellence and be able to describe what is happening at any moment in the lifecycle of the firm. The ability to extract meaningful and actionable insight from the data on operations, cash position, profit and loss, sales, marketing, and even aspects of the culture is paramount for success. Businesses must be conscious of how well every factor is mapping toward their strategic goals, budgets, and forecasts.

Two: Employ human-centric foresight generating practices such as Design Thinking and map out Sustaining, Disruptive, and Breakthrough innovations to gain or maintain a leadership position in the categories where you do business.

While insight is critical, without foresight a business will not sustain its own growth and will wither while trying to wrangle the last drops of life out of the entity.

Insights fuel management decisions and aid smart marketing. Foresight creates leaders who define what a category means. You need both or risk being operationally near- or far-sighted; however, foresight appears to be in short supply.

The Gold Left on the Table

We always feel badly for clients of a full-cycle innovation project. After the many ideation and co-creation sessions, there are far too many viable concepts to pursue. In many cases, millions of dollars of market expansion, new products with tested, validated appeal, and new licensing opportunities get swept aside just because there are too many possibilities.

While we have formulas for figuring out the right mix for a product line portfolio, far too many concepts never get their stage time on the market. Sometimes the products would transform the business from selling in one channel to selling in a different one. Other times a service brand could enter the market selling a hard product. Yet other times it is a revolution to a business model with investment risks—for example, a product-based company had a viable and feasible way to pilot test a service-based store that sold products. This move could have been the beginning to a franchising event that would have the potential to more than triple the growth. In another case a strong licensing partner could have taken a whole suite of new, branded products to a new market.

In all of these cases, gold is left on the table. All of the examples above hail from the myriad of our client mix, but it could equally well represent any firm with a serious innovation discipline.

Here's the question: who is responsible for the gold left on the table, the aftermarket of valuable ideas? Because if no one is, they will wither away in a Final Report and your organization will never harvest the total value of its innovation efforts.

Should Innovation-centric firms create a new role? A Gold Sweeper. This person would work with all the various departments to see that the most viable ideas get the stage time and consideration not allotted at most organizations. Furthermore, they can formally document all of the gold left on the table.

The amount of value that never sees the light of day can be the catalytic driver of growth, if there is a process and person dedicated to seeing tested and viable concepts make it to the market.

Beyond the Brainstorm

As a critical phase of any innovation project, ideation brings the generative possibilities to life. While there are similarities with traditional brainstorming, there are also some key differences. Let's explore both.

Both brainstorming and ideation are processes invented to create new valuable ideas, perspectives, concepts, and insights, and both are methods for envisioning new frameworks and systemic problem solving.

Both can be useful in every type of business, in the non-profit world, and in the public and social sectors. Both fall in the category of creative processes, though in fact they both are creative and scientific, just not linear. Ideation and brainstorming share some ground rules (generate as many ideas as possible, do not classify them at this stage as good or bad, one conversation at a time, for example). They share some exercises, such as Worst Idea Ever, leaving your day-job role out of the room, clustering, and more. They share many similar rules, courtesies, tactics, exercises, methods, and objectives.

Ideation, however, is not merely an eloquent variation of time-tested brainstorming. While brainstorming uses a variety of exercises to unlock new thinking about old subjects—and follows a trajectory of immersion, incubation, and insight generation – ideation is more visionary in nature, seeking to see and discern solutions for problems that are not yet defined in many cases.

Ideation also uses a variety of methods to reframe the fundamental mental model of a subject—think of seeing the same thing from different lenses—in order to see it anew. The concept of Sprints also stimulates the ideation session and also helps focus the intended scope within the parameters of a set time. Many of these sprints have built-in methods of building on other ideas and concepts inherent in the process.

Revenue Model Exercise

One generative exercise for any CPG company to explore growing market share is hold a session where a team role-plays a wide array of alternative revenue models for a particular brand.

As far as the ground rules for this ideation session, any ideas should be welcomed—and the cultural antibodies of HOW WE HAVE ALWAYS DONE THINGS need to be silenced. This session will not only challenge your existing model and inspire new, profitable thinking, but will also unlock new avenues of growth the existing paradigm of doing business usually will not allow considering.

We know what you're thinking: "our whole business is built around creating products and distributing them in certain channels by set, predictable methods." Don't worry. The feasibility of enacting one or more of these new growth areas can be vetted rigorously after the session. This workshop is for creating and surfeiting desirability.

Here are the eight revenue models to explore:

1. Unit Sales

2. Ad Fees

3. Franchise Fees

4. Utility Fees

5. Subscription Fees

6. Transaction Fees

7. Professional Fees

8. License Fees

Each of the eight models offers a multitude of ways to create sales or fees. Even thinking about your current model, take Unit Sales for example, with uninhibited gusto can lead you to discover new ways to drive sales, such as selling in different channels, creating a premium niche, displaying in different categories or departments, etc.

Once you have all of the output of the revenue model innovation exercise, your team can discern the most probable means to augment your existing revenue model. Whether the session yields a dramatic breakthrough or simply incremental growth that increases sales and brand value, this exercise is a worthwhile and cost-effective method of realizing more value within your current portfolio.

Turning Good Ideas into Great Products

One innovation method is to invite customers (in a B-2-B situation) or consumers (in a B-2-C scenario) into the creative process with you. Here, they will ideate, workshop concepts that arise in the session, augment concepts provided for them, and create some new product or service ideas that do not yet exist.

There are several forms of co-creation, and I will sketch out two here, as demonstrations of the method.

Category co-creation is where you explore categories and have a team explore and solve a problem from the widest frame possible, such as how do things in nature carry water. While it may sound unwieldy, such an exercise can unfetter the minds of engineers and product managers in the beverage, lotion, or related industries, resulting in a game-changing design.

Another form is concept co-creation, where you provide very crude (i.e., hand-drawn) concepts of new ways to approach an old problem and allow people to dialogue, and draw what would make this a better solution for them. This exercise can be used not only for hard products, but also for service experiences. In fact, Mayo Clinic used this method to great effect when redesigning their patient experience.

The premise of co-creation is to break the force-feeding "I like" and "I don't like" ratings of traditional market research. By inviting real users to create with you – and by often making real-time feedback on prototypes, companies can keep their hands on the pulse of what moves and inspires the people who use their products and services.

The real value of co-creation is the difference of having people rate a good idea and inviting relevant users into the alchemical process of working together to make a good idea into a breakthrough market opportunity. Co-creation helps to refine the working assumptions and hunches in the product design process, and the method also helps weed out pet ideas of the internal stakeholders, before they bomb in the market. By collaborating with the people for whom the solution is being designed, you get to a solution faster and often with more elegance.

While a lot of ideation work happens before the co-creation session, you also need to know that you may not get "the answer" in the session; however, you will gain deep insight, get real market feedback, and reframe the problem you are trying to solve.

Co-creation sessions add multiple points of value. Often, they unlock the code of growth that can make your company a category leader.

Shift Things Around

When leading a series of innovation workshops in our home town for the Mayor's Innovation Delivery Team with division leaders at Memphis' City Hall, our task was steep: change long-standing behavior patterns. Turn doers into innovators. Have proven professionals who are deeply imbedded in their roles get out of their current paradigm and empathize with the community and citizens they serve. Break the cognitive lock created by doing the same thing every day and see the city with fresh eyes.

While we created several fast-paced and role-playing exercises to accomplish this goal, we wanted to evoke the sense that this was not business as usual from the outset.

We arrived early to plan for the session. The space itself was set up for parliamentary-style debates. On the wall were daunting signs that read, "DO NOT MOVE THE FURNITURE." There was no choice but to break the mandate of City Hall.

To shift the roles, we had to shift the rules, respectfully and playfully. To change the space is to change the poetics of space. By altering the configuration of the room, we alter the expectations of the participants. Everything shifts.

When the division leaders entered and saw a space that once was set up for debate and competition now set up for playful collaboration and exploration, it was a clear sign that this would be not only a meeting, but an experience—and it was. Even the mayor stopped by and reveled in the workshop's findings and the animated level of potential in the room. The participants were energized, engaged, and an active, crucial part of the creative problem solving process.

The lesson: shift things around. Move people into new roles for a day or just a meeting. Move furniture. Change desks for a day. Experiment with breaking set patterns, for a limited time. Not only is it re-energizing for the participants, but it also yields beneficial insights that might grow a business or make the world a better place.

Next Step,
Innovate the Open Young Minds

One objective of the Memphis Innovation Bootcamp is to build a community of innovators. The more we socialize these methods and tools, the larger the social and business problems can be met with creativity, empathy, and the widest range of possible solutions.

Thus far, we have held mini bootcamps with companies, university and college students, and non-profits. The number of innovators is growing; however, the impact—thus far—is limited to product development and a little bit of city planning, thanks to our peers at the Memphis Mayor's Innovation Delivery Team.

No offense, but it is an almost insurmountable challenge to open the minds of career-track, socially-conditioned professionals to see the city through the lens of pure possibility. To remedy this business-centric application of innovation, we are making strides to take the Bootcamp to high schools, both public and private.

If we can teach Design Thinking to the emerging generation it will achieve many benefits, including: stopping the brain drain from the region, mixing multi-generational teams of volunteers working together to make the region a healthier and more vibrant community, seeing the region with eyes of potential, stimulating a culture renaissance, and, most important, teaching creativity and critical thinking to the generation who will inherit Memphis.

The impact of design thinking in education has two overarching, positive benefits: First, it insists upon a multi-disciplinary approach—design thinking demonstrates that bringing together seemingly disparate perspectives can be key to discovering effective solutions. Therefore, this approach shows students that the most complex problems are best solved using an interdisciplinary approach.

Second, the power of collaborating with others: design thinking emphasizes that through collaboration (rather than cut-throat competition) is critical to the learning and problem solving process—a mindset that will be valuable to their scholarly, professional, and personal lives.

But the real benefit is teaching the power of empathy with others. Design thinking teaches students that the best solutions are empathy-driven and created for real people with real problems. By understanding that an answer to a problem is only as good as the user finds it to be, students understand that solutions that really connect to others are more valuable than solely empirical or logic-based problem solving methodologies taught today.

The world is what we make it. Teaching students empathy, collaboration, and methods for being cunningly creative will empower the city for generations to come and inspire all of us to make it a better place instead of merely accepting the status quo as is.

Innovation, as a discipline, tends to be special assignment work that is reserved for the creative hotshots, iconoclasts, those in hot spots like Palo Alto, or on an esteemed university campus, such as M.I.T. Yet, the lack of a real practice of innovation cripples businesses and communities. The dirty secret is that *anyone* can do it with a little training.

Another secret is that innovation work and its methods are not competitive; rather, as a model, innovation holds the very keys to a collaborative, sustainable future for companies, non-profits, cities, and individuals. You just have to do it. Not talk about it, read about it, or speculate, but do. Action wins.

To this end, several peers in the community who are passionate about Innovation and its positive impact on business and the social sector started meeting to share their passion. The natural outgrowth was the Memphis Innovation Bootcamp. Organizations on the founding team included Merck, FedEx, University of Memphis, and the Southern Growth Studio.

The Design Thinking methods were adapted from Stanford's D. School. MIB is a three-day, intensive, hands-on introduction to the latest concepts in design thinking and innovation. We have held six sessions, founded an advisory board, and are building up an infrastructure of innovators who can get behind projects that make the region a better place. MIB is a three-day, intensive, hands-on introduction to the latest concepts in design thinking and innovation.

Mission of Memphis Bootcamp

Create a network of innovators who produce human-centered solutions that positively transform lives, communities, and businesses.

Approach

MIB – A 3 day hands-on, real-world, exciting, transformative immersion experience that imparts application-ready design thinking capability.

MIB Connect – MIB connects local businesses, organizations and governments with local and global resources, to establish a network of robust Design Thinking programs.

MIB Engage – MIB staff engages with a select group of local organizations to impact the community and help establish Design Thinking capability.

Think of it as a Memphis Innovation Revolution or innovation for the rest of us.

Alas, Poor Henry and the Problem

According to legend, Henry Ford scoffed at market research and what we now call Consumer Insights, proclaiming, "If I had asked people what they wanted, they would have said faster horses." While there is a certain degree of wisdom in this statement, it has been misquoted to justify bad, hubris-inspired product failures by too many corporate egos.

Yes, to Ford's credit, sometimes the visionary impulse of the inventor lives outside of convention. However, Ford made a mistake by thinking of his customers as unimaginative drones and an objectified, uncreative herd.

In reality, this quote is an act of fiction and cannot be traced back to the writings or sayings of Henry Ford. Ford was too smart and too shrewd to ignore customers or to act like a tone-deaf, singularly gifted inventor. He knew his audience – and this insight drove him to find ways to design a process that enabled the vision of an affordable car for the masses. The key to success and good design that wins in the market: knowing your audience.

If you give people a chance – and also employ formal discovery, ideation, and brainstorming processes and methods – they can help your company define the real problems in the market. You have to let consumers or customers (if you are a B2B company) co-create with you to identify the unmet needs and their real desires. After you understand their world and their perspectives, you can validate these findings with a mix of empirical, observational, and even intuitive modes and methods.

The real key to creating a disruptive, breakthrough innovation is discernment. By knowing the context of the people in the market, you know the gaps. In these gaps dwell the seeds of future market leadership.

The issue is one of orientation. If you approach an innovation project or a venture with a rigid, fixed notion of what the market needs, and you have not actually bothered to check with the market, you have paid a great disrespect. You have also created a wall between you and reality. You are creating in a vacuum.

Consumer or customer insights can help your company define the real needs and design a wildly new solution that solves a human problem.

So, if you walk into a new product meeting and the pipeline manager begins by saying "Henry Ford said ... ," just laugh, tell him or her that you find the brazen notion amusing and you appreciate the creative thrust that birthed the product concept; however, we need to test the need and validate that it is a problem the market will pay for.

Here, your customers can give you visceral context of what the market will or will not accept. Letting them back up into problem solving around the market need will give you many more product concepts. A few of these ideas may be pure gold.

Allow Innovation Exercises
to Expand Business Model

As your innovation efforts begin to move from the ideation to the testing phase, or the co-creation with consumers or customers, outlandish and disruptive concepts present themselves. As messy as children arriving, they show up, saying "feed me, let me scream at the top of my lungs, I'm uncivilized" all without speaking.

Don't be put off by how wild or unconventional they may be at first. Remember, breakthrough thinking sits right next to insanity, or as we in the trade say, "awesome sits right next to ridiculous."

Instead of having a knee-jerk overreaction to something novel, practice non-judgment on some of your discernment filters. Even if the concepts do not fit your current business model that doesn't mean you cannot capitalize on the insight in a number of ways.

Here are three viable models to consider whereby you can realize the value of the more seemingly "out there" innovations that arise as a natural part of the process.

First, if the market seems big enough and you have resources to deploy, start a new branch of your business. This could mean a product company selling as a subscription rather than at retail, or starting an e-commerce only channel for a specific product. Or, it could mean a service business launching a product line. Or, a product company could pilot a store with an eye to growing it into a franchise business.

Second, maybe you can license your brand to a key partner for this particular concept. You've already developed the idea and completed market testing on it, and therefore have a realistic grasp on the market desirability and technical feasibility. Make sure this scenario is a win-win—that your partner has something to gain and also already has something key that you do not, whether it be channel distribution or technological expertise. A good licensing partner can make a good concept a great success.

Third, think brand marriage. Find a good relationship with a brand that makes a good marriage. Think of Cole Haan using Nike insoles or Apple using Intel chips. So many examples come to mind where the best of each company becomes part of a whole offering.

The main thesis here is don't toss away good concepts because they don't fit your existing business model. If you invest the time and energy, you can reap a bigger harvest than your current paradigm allows. Think broadly.

Add Financial Elements Early in the Innovation Process

Innovation is a saturated field, but one with a hole in it. Many companies can generate thousands of potentially valuable ideas, but have no acceptable cultural method for placing a value on them.

Many of these same companies can do Wicked Thinking, block out Business Model Canvases, and follow a Design Thinking Sprint, but they lack credible and concrete thinking about the financial side of their innovation concepts as the front-end process is progressing.

Too many in the innovation field do not translate their findings into their company's existing vernacular. As a result, they don't get buy-in from the people who take them to market and they wither on the vine.

Good marketers and product managers speak the language of money. Therefore, even if you've followed a strict human-centric method of innovation, speaking about the end-game will help socialize the efforts.

Invite the business side of the house into the project cycle earlier to gain their buy-in. By looking at each major step in the process through a financial lens, you will win their trust. Here are a few methods.

After you have completed the Empathy and Define stages, invite them into a Business Model exercise, so they get a sense of the pragmatism of the process. To boot, they also earn a real sense of the problem for which you are solving.

After the Ideation phase is complete and you present the concepts, add some thinking about how the concept will be monetized and why it is important for the brand.

During co-creation present each concept with features, benefits, and also test pricing.

As the Front End process is wrapping up, present each vetted product or service concept with a one-page *draft* business case and suggested *go-to-*

market brief.

Adding these Back End elements to the Front End process creates a bridge between the Innovation and Business Team. By applying these simple tactics to the process, more innovations actually make it to market.

The Back End of Innovation

The Back End of Innovation

Many CEOs say that they have more growth ideas than they know what to do with. It seems like there is a universal love affair with generating ideas but less enthusiasm when it comes to figuring out which ideas are the most commercially viable and how to actually implement.

This imbalance causes a backlog of ideas, begging the question: Do too many ideas stall out innovation?

This quandary is rooted in what is known as the "Frontend of Innovation," which is the idea generation part of the process, and the "Backend of Innovation," which is the strategy and implementation of these ideas.

Companies with an established innovation program have these two elements in balance. Innovation stalls out when there is a bandwidth issue — either there are no analysts on staff to evaluate each opportunity or there are too few of them and, like the patent officers at the USPTO, they never see the light of day.

As much as we love the creative idea generation process, we are also keenly aware that ideas are a dime a dozen. Extensive market validation is needed to prioritize, incubate, and develop the concepts with the most legs. Just like with a startup, market validation means proving (or disproving) feasibility, demand, and profitability.

Singular devotees of the Frontend of Innovation hate talking about this reality, it makes their skin crawl. This is because putting these limitations in people's minds during ideation limits the creative output and perhaps blocks a breakthrough. We agree, but with generative ideation and limited validation it is easy to see how the backlog ensues. Without a quantitative way to gauge ideas, they can all appear equally appealing.

So now, we will give the Backend of Innovation a rare moment in the spotlight. It doesn't get a lot of airtime because it is the less glamorous workhorse of the innovation process, but without it, innovation suffocates from idea overcrowding. Much like the tired funnel diagram, the Backend sets up a process and framework to assess ideas and eliminate the weakest from the development pipeline.

Market size, consumer insights, competitive pressure, business model, and return on investment are just the beginning of the factors that should be assessed before moving the concept forward to pilot.

Figure out what other factors are critical go/no-go stage gates for your organization to narrow the funnel. The basic questions are: How big is the market? What is the competitive pressure and does this represent a better alternative? Does the end user want and accept this solution? What is the business model, and what are the operational factors involved?

Strive for the intersection of generative and lucrative. As with many things in life, the key is balance and moderation.

Business Case, Selling Internally & Proof of Concept in the Market

Measuring Innovation with Money

Innovation is such a heady, ill-defined concept. Innovation is one of those words – like strategy or creativity – that means either nothing or something different to anyone who hears it. But when handled correctly, genuine innovations are the lifeblood of any company's continued health and success.

How do genuine innovations get measured?

Money.

Revenue and profit. Cold, hard cash. Top-line growth. Money.

Many innovation methods have stopgap checkpoints for seeing the financial potential. Our favorite is loosely based on a seven-question grid created by the authors of the Business Model Canvas. We will share its basic insights herein, as the Southern Growth Studio uses it as a starting point for judging the monetary potential of breakthrough innovations (not cost-saving or incremental innovations; however, those are measured by different metrics).

When vetting a breakthrough innovation ensure it meets at least one of these criteria. The more the better.

Switching Costs – does your innovation make it difficult to switch to a competitor? In a plain-speaking analogy, are you easy to wed and hard to divorce?

Recurring revenue – how does cash flow? Hopefully on an ongoing basis from each customer.

Earn before you spend – can you get an order without being too capital intensive? Think about Dell in its heyday, how the company changed the game by not assembling computers until orders were placed.

Game-changing cost structure – can you change the whole way an industry operates? Can you be a Netflix against Blockbuster? Change the game.

Getting others to do the work – can you enroll others to help you add value? What is Facebook without all of the many, willing users who create all the content?

Scalability – is there ample room to multiply growth in the market without too many costs added?

Protecting from competition – is your concept defensible in one way or another?

After doing the necessary field, empathy, definition, and ideation work, get your innovation team to vet their breakthrough concepts against these seven questions. If they pass at least one, green light the prototype and test, test, and refine.

Did we mention that money will follow?

Enroll the Skeptics Early

After working on hundreds of innovation projects, one fact remains. If you cannot get executive sponsorship of the final concepts, they will never launch. We recommend a few steps to get leadership engaged in solving the problem with you as part of the process. Therefore, they will feel invested in the outcome of the innovations in the marketplace.

Set up a meeting to unpack the starting assumptions of the Innovation Project. Make sure you include time to think about unthinkable things. For example, if the company needs a new product, make sure you include time to ideate on different business models. Also, provide the context to free everyone of their current paradigm and boundaries.

We like to use a simple exercise called What Will Get Us Fired, and we encourage wild thinking. Have your team begin by thinking about all types of illicit, weird, and shadowy things they are not allowed to voice normally. Then, make their minds stretch into solutions thinking. Have them pair up, pick the wildest ones, and then flip the concepts on their head, and transform them into a concept the market would accept. Once they witness the process, they will understand that awesome breakthroughs often sit right next to ridiculous.

Then, re-write their role. Instead of setting them up to analyze the results at the end of the process in a PASS/FAIL or YES/NO dynamic, have them check in as part of a team invested in something that will enhance the company's top line and make it brand a leader. Call them an Action Team or a Realization Team, something inherently collaborative and additive.

Check in at key points. After all of the Empathy and fieldwork is complete, give them a window into the insights. Likewise, after the Define phase is complete, connect the dots for them, let them help wordsmith the reframing of the findings so they have genuine ownership in solving the right problem.

Use their expertise. Let's say one member is in the legal department, one is in RnD, one is in business development, and another works in regulatory affairs. After the Ideation phase is complete and consumer desirability has been validated for concepts in a series of prototype Co-Creations, then enroll them at their level of expertise by asking them to help figure out how to make these possible solutions technically feasible and market viable. We have witnessed naysayers transformed into complex problem solvers on the widest array of issues: chemistry, technology, claims work, etc.

Many members of this group are pre-amped to say "no, here is why it won't work," and this habitual knee-jerk response has caused billions of dollars to be left on Innovation's cutting room floor. By getting their enrollment early, and by making them part of the process and solution, they work toward, rather than against, new products and solutions.

Measure Twice, Cut Once

Ideas are a dime a dozen, indeed; the old cliché holds true. When following a formal Innovation process, it pays to measure the size of the market potential and validate the concept before investing in a build.

To investors and shareholders, an endless proliferation of ideas signals a lack of strategy and desperation. Unmeasured ideas without serious market validation lack merit. After the idea generation or ideation phase is formally closed, it is time to put on the analytical hat.

Too many ideas are worse than the common cold for a fast-growing business. New product and service ideas can paralyze, confuse, or even constrict growth.

Ideas flow too freely to some entrepreneurs and driven executives. In our experience, many of the brainstormers are too busy to discern an idea's true value. Often, they lack the expertise and patience to nurture an idea into its full market potential.

As the shiny new things, novel ideas can distract a company's real mission and operational effectiveness – and dilute hard-earned, long-term brand equity if a new product or service gets launched that cheapens the company's reputation.

Yet, there might be authentic monetizing magic in an idea, a seed of real growth. How can you tell? Measure. Validate. Do the hard work of doing your homework.

It is not an idea itself, but the successful execution of a worthy idea that makes a measurable difference. Capturing an idea, vetting its value, and refining it into a leading product or service - that is the process by which an idea becomes worth many dozens of dimes.

Genuine innovation requires a pragmatic process. This is the real work, the boring part. Critical decisions need to be made early on with an unflinching eye. Include stage gates in the process where a concept may be killed if it does not meet muster.

The next time someone tells you that "ideas are cheap," agree with them, then pull out your spreadsheets, competitive studies, customer feedback reports, and market-validating research for your big idea.

If there is sound proof and a compelling plan, your idea may be market ready. For every idea that may have merit, apply the carpenter's rule: measure twice, then cut once.

Pilot & Market Test

Financial Speedbumps for Innovation

The creative process of birthing breakthrough innovations can provide a substantial top-line boon but it too often suffers a fatal flaw felt in failed product launch after failed product launch.

Welcome to the Innovation Graveyard. Hundreds of millions of dollars get lost here.

Most innovations fail because they don't get buy-in from the people who take them to market at key points in the process – and in words that motivate them. These marketers and product managers speak the language of money.

Find ways to build bridges with a larger pool of stakeholders to ensure the financial return of a firm's innovation investment, as well as practical tips and exercises for getting a sense of what innovations will make at each point in the innovation process.

This larger audience includes every product manager, research and development professional, product marketer, and innovation professional, as well as the directors, vice presidents, and C-level leadership who are responsible for the budgets and outcomes of the innovation efforts they sponsor.

They will care because they will be able to bridge the language of design and innovation with the language of business. Furthermore, use concrete tools, exercises and ways to model out and validate the expected financial return of each effort. As concepts move from the abstract to market-ready, we will offer ways to measure both the possible and probable returns.

This validation process is missing in the innovation frameworks today. By adding this set of tools the business side of the house will become enrolled and energized into the innovation process earlier. Their involvement is the key to winning in the market.

Lastly, we recommend employing a few critical Go/No Go decision-making tools, and a few quick instruments for prioritizing large numbers of possible innovations.

In the end, companies can have more assurance with their innovation spending and make decisions based on what innovations have the best chance of making money.

Most of the exercises noted here complement one another and can be used together to craft a full business case and go-to-market strategy at the end of the process.

Market Power Verses Brute Force

Pushing too hard?

Rushing to hit short-term numbers or an over-caffeinated executive can force some costly mistakes.

Failed product launches. A weak but bloated product pipeline. A service in desperate need of reinvention but too entrenched and in love with its own methods to change. A company that charges ahead blindly, carrying dead weight and a dying value proposition to the market. A feature set that doesn't meet users real needs. Add a bomb from your professional experience here _____. There are too many mistakes to name.

There are also too many forced agendas, pet projects, products and services zealously guarded by the ego patrols and sycophants. The world is already overstuffed with such glut. Do us all a favor, stop forcing things to happen just because you feel so motivated.

There is a critical difference between force and authentic market power. Force helped birth the Industrial Revolution, but is a brutish, blunt, and inelegant way to finish anything in business today. Real market power shares the verities of wisdom: self-knowledge, a sense of others, and the ability to read between the lines and see a real need, an actual benefit for your product or service.

Market power creates fans, brand evangelists, and loyalty. Market power always finds traction in the field by connecting with its intended audiences in both fundamentally expected and wildly unexpected ways. This type of power can be measured with sales, brand equity, and breakout potential.

On the other hand, when things are forced, you find yet another company for sale, more products at the closeout store, and disgruntled employees.

Why force anything today when the world has too many choices to begin with? Instead, get real market power by empathizing with customers and crafting something of real and usable value to their lives.

Go away, brute. Your tricks don't work anymore.

Naming the Baby:
Product Naming 101

If you ask business experts what is the most fundamental ingredient in a successful product launch, you may hear three things: distribution, quality, or pricing. All three are merely givens in this era—mandatory.

But what really makes a difference?

The real competitive advantage for a new product is its name. Likewise, a bad name can sink a good product like a stone thrown into a lake.

A strong name that conveys the emotional essence of a product's value can improve sales, create a brand that grows in long-term value, and quickens first-time purchases. A bad name can kill a product during the launch phase. In fact, a good name acts as a calling card in the world, instead of a source of shame, confusion, or indifference.

Yet, product names are sometimes created for wrong reasons or are off target for the intended market.

Let's examine a loser before we look at a simple framework. Ask Audi about their TT. You could just as likely ask any kindergartener about their TT and get the same response.

What self-respecting driver wants to sit behind the wheel of a TT?

Absurd! Idioms matter. Be careful for the traps of translation, too. When Colgate introduced a toothpaste in France called *Cue*, it may have proven comical with readers of the porn magazine of the same name, but no-one else.

Think of successful naming as including both sound and sense. The sonic values have to work, as does the sense making given the dynamics of culture, nationalities, and the competitive landscape.

There are many factors to consider: positioning, market trends and drivers, translation issues, URL availability, more.

Product naming should be done justice in either a long essay or book on the subject; however, here is a short take.

First off, know your enemy. Look at the competitive landscape and make sure you are not naming a me-too product. Aim to be wholly your own. The key is to be different, unique, and helpful.

Secondly, the best names are literal and poetic at the same time, like Office or Raid. Tapping both the descriptive and figurative sides of the brain with one name makes it resound and resonate with denotative and connotative value.

Third, short is best. TT may be the exception to this rule; it's bad for other reasons.

Fourth, don't suffer feature mania. A simple, non-technical name that conveys the end promise or benefit is always more effective than a name that describes a feature.

Fifth, use a name that evokes some emotional resonance in the audience and rewards their use of the product.

Mostly, avoid really bad mistakes like Poolife, which reads more like Poo Life than Pool Life. Use good judgment and be smart.

Inside Your Company

Courage

As Innovation and Growth Strategy consultants we have methods, processes, and exercises that we apply to client problems. While tools from this vast toolbox work for any type of organization seeking to provide a better service or product (healthcare, non-profit, hospitality, consumer goods, financial services, wholesalers, and B-2-B) to generate insights and custom solutions that set them up as a category leader, what we sell is something else ultimately. This is perhaps the rarest asset in corporate America for an unknown reason, called courage.

According to Wikipedia, Courage is the ability and willingness to confront fear, pain, danger, uncertainty, or intimidation. Most corporate cultures move in fear, make decisions for the worst case, then present power points for their leadership teams like a pep rally squad playing the roles of analyst and accountant. What happened to the ability to dream, to share a vision, to outline something bold? In the land of how-we-do-things-here, no new thinking is allowed and courage is stamped out the moment it shows the glint in its dreamy eye.

It's little wonder that all of the big telecommunications companies can only grow by major acquisition rather than human invention. Given that they are fixed and rigid in their business model, infrastructure costs, and roles, they cannot afford to re-think the industry. So, in moves a concept that defies their paradigmatic models, Skype, and without the capital-intensive notion of a network, they become the market leader in international calls with more than 12% of the market. The bigger companies lacked the courage to drop their world-view and see the market needs and new technological possibilities with the objectivity of a start-up.

Yet, many corporate citizens lust after such a wild leap. On every corporate desk we see copies of the *Business Model Canvas* or *Lean Start-up*.

Skunkworks teams meet with the fervor and passion of illicit love. Like stolen love, these relationships rarely make it in the light of day. The concepts are cleaned up and presented to the larger enterprise. Then, behold the attack. Behold the boundaries. Behold the reasons why we cannot move ahead with something radical. Faint praise for fresh thinking peppers the conversation, then it's back to business as usual.

This cynical, but too-true, scene is enacted again and again every day in America. Cultural antibodies eat at any expression of courage like rapacious piranhas in company after company. The only antidote is courage, the courage to confront fears, dangers, and uncertainties. To be able to enact this courage, it takes a focus on an innovation culture where even the business model that brings us together is an on-going experiment and prototype open to improvement.

Courage; it changes things, for the better.

The Role of Culture

Michael Graber 99

The (Fill in the Blank) Way

Each professional entity has a way of handling business. This way is encoded with spoken and codified rules and unspoken and non-verbal clues on how to perform. What gets done, how decisions are made, and how money is allocated can be defined as "culture." This way, then, is an explicit and implicit set of rituals that reward or punish based on its own complicated, internal logic.

This way, the culture, has adapted over the years. Still, this way is now a well-defined machine of productivity. It weeds out unfitting talent and risks, and it refines work and the flow of work to a crystalline precision. This way creates a shorthand, and saves money, time, and preserves the sense of the place.

Think about it for a minute. What is your organization's way for handling presentations, new product decisions, new market assessments, service issues, or resolving conflicts? What are the processes, check points, keys to enrollment, and styles of presentation that have become the default way in your organization? How are people rewarded or punished?

Now, do yourself and your organization a valuable favor. Acknowledge that this way is only an agreed upon construction of reality, a mental model and not reality itself.

Here is why: noticing the norms of a model, a way, and then consciously unlearning some of its defaults are key steps in taking breakthrough, disruptive innovations to the market.

You see, every culture has antibodies built into the system. New ideas are typically rejected as vehemently as foreign objects are rejected by the body. The _____ way may be your biggest obstacle. Therefore, you have to develop the visionary ability to zoom out and get a real sense of the market potential of a new business concept without the blinding shackles of "how we do it today" to limit the thinking.

Sure, there is a time for risk assessment, validation, and a synthesis period of how we, as the _____ way, take this completely new line of business in a channel to market, but if you don't cultivate this keen zooming out ability, the culture will not allow you to dream valuable dreams.

Remember, those who are called to innovate have to be systems thinkers and visionaries. Luckily, both are learnable skills. The factor that stymies innovation most is the unconscious defaults of a company culture. Those who recognize the system's operating assumptions and gently inspire others to stretch their thinking on behalf of the organization change the culture in countless positive ways.

The Innovation Process: What's the Secret Sauce?

Business banter talks a lot about "the process for innovation," which is usually referenced in the singular and stated definitively, leaving most business leaders scratching their heads. It makes us think that there is one correct process, the secret sauce that top companies have and follow. There are actually thousands of innovation processes, none of which have been quantified or proven to be the most effective. There is no one size fits all.

There is also no secret sauce. Most companies attempt an ad hoc innovation approach without clearly defined roles and processes, then suffer mixed results. Company leaders hear so much about this all-important but ever-elusive business imperative. They look for the fabled innovation handbook then become overwhelmed by the many innovation gurus, each with a unique system.

Innovation just means trying something new in your market to better meet your customers' needs, thus driving growth for your company. It's making a change rather than just doing the same thing better.

How do I do this in a sensible way that mitigates my risk, you ask? The key is to develop a process that works for your company and will stick. It's just like a diet – if it is not a behavioral and physiological fit, it will never work. Keep in mind that culture plays a big role here. If your company has an old-timer mentality that rejects any form of change, then your first step is to retool the culture. Don't expect to transform your company's culture into Google. There is no magic formula for this. You need to find your own way. Strive to become a smarter, more nimble, and more opportunistic version of your former culture. Assume a proactive mindset, strive to lead the industry rather than react to it.

When your team is in the right frame of mind, figure out who is in charge and clearly define roles. One of the secrets to a good innovation process is making it iterative. Think about using the following tools at multiple points in the process:

- End user feedback: what are their pain points? Where is the demand?
- Market segment size and saturation level.
- Trend spotting and scenario planning.
- Ideation: expand your team's thinking with interactive exercises to generate new ideas.
- Design thinking: visually represent and design solutions for market pain points. Use empathy for the context of a problem, creativity in the generation of insights and solutions, and rationality to analyze and fit solutions to the context.
- Stage gates: go/no-go criteria at critical points in the process.
- Prototype and test ideas with actual users, get them to co-create the solutions with you.

Make this a discipline not a diversion. Put receptivity to change and discipline in your secret sauce. The market leaders cook with this. Turn up the heat and you can too.

The Happy Virus

We'll preface this section with an unconventional source of wisdom for business, the great Persian poet Hafiz:

The Happy Virus
I caught the happy virus last night
When I was out singing beneath the stars.
It is remarkably contagious - So kiss me.

In business there is no greater asset than an inspired culture. Such environments create a Happy Virus that leads to optimized bottom lines and thriving top-line growth. Happy viruses that infiltrate top-performing cultures happen when strategy becomes manifested in the culture.

Despite recent books, articles, and decent debate over Culture Trumping Strategy, this war of culture versus strategy is a one-sided and misguided notion.

Business cultures that have The Happy Virus do not exist in spite of strategy. The opposite point holds true. Vibrant business cultures are a result of having and manifesting a strategy that resonates within the organization and in the market. Culture does not exist without strategy.

Ponder how cultures are built. It is a three-step process of bringing an entity into being that is as old as the human psyche: thought, word, and deed.

First a thought is formed. In business, the thought that births a venture usually fills a market need and is also aspirational. As Steve Jobs encouraged, such thoughts need to have passion enough to "put a dent in the universe." All businesses begin with thought. Then, do your homework.

You put your vision—the thought—into words. This is the strategic phase. This strategy provides a blueprint for building your business and crafting the right kind of culture that can birth and sustain a growing business.

The kind of culture you have is a result of how well you have manifested and managed your strategy. The deed phase becomes the culture itself.

Because the lifecycle of business is dynamic, this three-part process—thought, word, and deed—needs to be reviewed and adapted annually.

Culture, once established, can sustain a business that has lost touch of its core strategic thrust for a short time. Culture cannot make up for a lack of strategy.

The companies that know that a vibrant culture is a result of a founding vision and a smart, up-to-date strategy that becomes explicit and manifested into the hearts and minds of its employees and the market embody The Happy Virus. It's contagious in the best way—and it's the CEO's job to ensure that this benign and magnificent virus take root. Such thinking has worked for luminaries such as Richard Branson, Max De Pree, Anita Roddick, and others.

If you can put thought, word, and deed into a single focus and manifest your strategy into a palpable culture, you can be a market leader.

Creativity Redefined for Innovation

The words "creative" and "creativity" have been hi-jacked by the world of advertising. The word means something specific to those familiar with *Mad Men* or *Thirty-something* advertising stereotypes. In these cases – and the cases of classic advertising – creativity was visual, copy, or positioning cleverness applied at the end of the new product process, when it was time to market downstream.

The old view of the world buffers creativity from strategy or strategic planning or research and development. These departments were once reserved for eggheads, chemists, number crunchers, or analysts. If "creativity" were enacted in these functional areas, the deliverables and output would be suspect or suspended.

We are learning that creativity is anything that adds value and relevance to its intended audience. Smart companies are finding ways to move away from the Just-build-it-like-I-told-you model. They are discovering that the merely deductive way of handling strategy or R&D has more limitations than benefits.

To move more effectively downstream, companies are learning to be more creative upstream. This move signifies that we have moved out of the Industrial Era and into the Age of Innovation.

Upstream creativity means that companies immerse themselves with their customers and seek to invent helpful products and services. Upstream creativity means that the core business model is debated annually in different formats – and not just on a spreadsheet – intuitive downloads, sketches of new adaptations of the model, and market trends are role played as part of the new process. Upstream creativity means that there are markers and sticky notes in the boardrooms and executive chambers. Upstream creativity is a dynamic process that adapts to grow, takes calculated risks, and expects total engagement from its whole team.

The spirit of deep play can be found at such companies. The process of being creative for the sake of the business is a thrill and a form of bliss; peak moments in a career. Here, diverse project teams meet at the same table without prejudice about roles. They are intently focused on surprising the market by creating a new line of business that will change the game. They journey together through the discovery, the birth of a new concept, the drafting of a business case, and the path to market.

Inspired companies allow recursive thinkers to challenge, inspire, even provoke anything too status quo that inhibits growth. Creativity means looking through as many lenses of a prism of the same issue as possible.

Here's the bottom line. The world has changed. The economy is now led by organizations that invent on a rapid, reoccurring basis.

In the Industrial Era, creativity was used as a means to differentiate products downstream. Now, in the Age of Innovation, the only way to win in the market is to get creative with the whole business: business model, R&D, distribution, etc.

"Creative" once described people with drafting boards who reeked of ink. Now, it is an honorific worthy of a pinstripe suit-wearing MBA grad in finance.

Welcome back, Creativity. You have been missed on many floors of business for too long. Upstream. Downstream. All around. Creativity is good for business and is worthy of praise.

OMB: Symptom of Business Sickness

Is your business haunted by the blinding ghosts that worked in another era?

The wealthiest man in Japan, Tadashi Yanai, has a business plan that looks 300 years into the future, but allows for annual updates as a matter of course. To date, he's worth more than $6 billion.

This testament to making what is unseen visible begs the question: why aren't others planning and building according to plan?

Does your business have a real plan that gets updated each year? Hearsay speculates that less than 10% of all businesses are managed according to a plan that is more comprehensive than an annual set of target numbers. This is a problem.

Yet, we are all rich beyond our wildest imaginings: each human is endowed with 18 million brain cells. Most people and most businesses do not perform the necessary processes to attune this innate gift to their personal or business advantage.

It is a visionary act to craft a plan and it takes supreme discipline to review it each year. Vision and discipline together provide the courage to endure and keep working toward success despite setbacks and obstacles.

Many of the companies suffer from a lack of vision and discipline. As a result they are not growing. Here are several red flags:

1. "We don't have a five year plan. We don't have a five month plan."
2. "Our revenue line has been the same for the past five years."
3. "Our industry is all me-too, so we just copy what's hot and get a little piece of that trend."

It doesn't matter if it is a manufacturing company, an importing concern, a logistics firm, or a software business. This lack of vision relegates these businesses to react to the market. Instead of defining a new paradigm for their industries, they choose to wither, lose market share, and move further away from a leading position.

Even worse, without a plan companies make decisions based on what worked a decade or two decades ago, even though the rest of the world has moved on. OBM is a ghost that not only haunts businesses that do not have the discipline to revise a strategic plan each year. OBM also depletes ingenuity and vigor of a firm, keeping its head blindly in the past. OBM means Old Business Model.

You can spot OBMs everywhere. It looks like the call center business whose customers have stated that they prefer email to phone calls, but metrics keep employees working the phones and alienating customers. Every business has to shed some aspects of its OBMs to stay present and add value to their client base.

Mister Yanai doesn't need to worry about OBMs because he has both a plan and vision that keep him focused, humble, and growing. He has the certainty of a plan and the agility of adapting the plan each year. Yanai stays upbeat, takes ups and downs in stride. He claims, "I might look successful but I've made many mistakes. People take themselves too seriously. You have to be positive and believe you will find success next time."

Good Manners and Innovation

Brainstorming sessions can easily devolve into a contest of strong egos or a parade of old, tired ideas and their accompanying resentments. Worse, meetings around ideation or innovation sour when there is lack of good manners.

Like roommates coming to terms on who cleans what and when, applying a few, simple house rules on the front end preserves relationships and creates a harmony in the environment.

Discipline is the handmaiden to creativity. You have to give the creative process a framework, basic parameters, to harness its value. Setting the house rules gives you the power to make something outside of pre-programmed egos in the room, something that may make you a market leader.

So, how do you manage this oh-so-human-tendency to dominate with the timeless cornerstone of civilization, good manners?

These manners often have to be imposed externally as social reinforcements to do the right thing instead of acting heedlessly on our own blinding passions in a creative frenzy.

The manners become house rules from generating a profusion of ideas. At this stage, research proves true again and again, the more ideas created the more valuable. So, the idea isn't to analyze each embryonic concept at this stage, but to create a trusting environment that allows for maximum idea creation.

Here are several examples of manners that can be used to create an effective innovation environment.

First, use good manners. This means doing what your mother should have told you. Don't interrupt. Have only one conversation going at any time. Listen respectfully. Don't judge. Don't bring your unruly pets (old ideas and rigid notions) to the party. Create a sense of trust.

Second, silence the inner editor. This is not the time to analyze or criticize, as natural as that impulse may be. Creativity is a process. Killing an idea before it has time to take its first breath and develop is akin to being a schoolyard bully. Leave your ego at the door. Be vulnerable and have fun.

Third, trust the process. There will be several steps in the process that will merit further exploration of a concept, so apply patience. More will be revealed, if you allow the generative creativity. A moderator will guide this discovery through a series of formal exercises designed for this process.

We could get more elaborate and craft a Ten Commandments of Innovation, but why? This move may inhibit the joy and outcome of the process. Stay simple.

Keep in mind that this a session where creativity and good manners will work hand-in-glove to generate a wealth of fresh thinking.

Why Experts Live in Fear

More trouble has fallen upon companies that tempt the universe with this ego-inflated statement: "We are the experts." A sizable lack of innovation occurs in the practice of being perceived as experts instead of practicing humility in the workplace.

What's wrong with admitting that you have a little to learn? What's wrong with keeping a fresh perspective on market and industry matters? Why such fear?

There is a stranglehold that takes hold when fear of not being an expert strikes a culture. While it's human nature to want to look smart in front of peers, acting like you know something you do not is simply immature. Acting as if your view of a reality is Reality is a woeful case of prideful ignorance on display.

When fear of not being an expert takes root in a corporate culture, it permeates every level of an enterprise. For professionals, there is the simple fear of not knowing the industry, terms, products, protocols, and people. For managers it is the fear of not being in the know of trends and players in the industry. At the director and VP levels, there runs amuck a fear of not being seen as an expert inside the organization. At the C-level the fear of having to change the core business focus and business model shuts down all exploration of the unknown.

All of these fears collectively form blind spots and a myopic point-of-view, allowing faster-growing, more nimble and open-minded competitors to arise out of nowhere and transform the industry.

Think about these examples. Blockbuster and Video-on-Demand, Netflix, and Redbox. After investing in real-estate and a business model that penalized customers, three disruptions quickly put the giant in its grave. Blockbuster's inflexibility, due to its "expertise" in the market, kept doing the actions that alienated customers.

Or consider Yahoo's portals. Yes, you can customize all the information you want into a large, overwhelming, and single dashboard, but can the brain really process that much information at once? Yes, said their "experts" until streamlined, simple, one-task focused search engines like Google drove their market share down to a public stage of crisis after a crisis that humbled them to get out of their Expert position and transform themselves serially.

Anything that lives is dynamic. Customers, competitors, the market itself move at the speed of life. The first step is admitting that you don't know everything. The second step is listening to those who use your product or services deeply. Then, when the Expert-ism fades, you find yourself in an authentic growth position.

Doing Right is Good Marketing.

Here is a short list of rapid cultural changes: Consumer and business databases. Cable. TIVO and DVR. The Internet. Search engines. Satellite radio. Podcasts. Social networks. Blogs. Mobile. The iPhone. Thousands more innovations in beta today.

The vehicles of marketing have transformed more in the last 10 years than in the previous 100 years. The communication tools and methods of the Industrial Era do not work in our shared world of instant information exchange.

Anyone and everyman has the power to publish either a confidential company memo or an opinion about your product or service with staggering ease.

It does not pay to be a communications dinosaur in the age of social utilities, blogs, and mobile connectedness. If your marketing team does not stay current, your marketing may do your company more harm than good.

Take Wal-Mart's recent healthcare public relations mishaps as an example. On one hand, the public one, the retail giant acknowledged that healthcare was the foremost reputational factor facing the company. They vowed to do well by doing good.

Then, an employee leaked an internal memo. Within hours, it zoomed across the Internet. In essence, the message implied that managers needed to fire the sick and aging. The company lost credibility across the globe at a time when it needed it most. The lesson: act in accord with your message. Let's call it Do Right Marketing.

Do what you say

In this era of transparency, companies best do what they say. Changes in technology sharpen how customers research, compare and choose to engage a company or buy a product. This news is true for consumer goods companies, business-to-business firms and service businesses.

Buyers judge your company with more access to information and opinion than in any time in history. As the old folksong states, "you better get your business fixed right."

Marketing is no longer about screaming "buy now" downstream with a pretty face and memorable expression. In fact, marketing now spawns back upstream to test the core principles of a business. My advice: apply the carrot rather than the stick.

Actual value

Instead of playing a communications shell game, invest your executive energies bringing actual value to the world. Provide something useful and then offer an enriching, on-going dialogue to your customers or clients. They are worth it.

Whether your marketing is created in-house or by an outsourced firm or a mix of employees and vendors, ensure that everyone who touches your marketing knows your company values, the power of social media and blogging and the importance of keeping your corporate actions and words in sync. Generations X and Y have a keen nose for sniffing out hypocrites. They vote against them with their wallets and expose them as frauds.

Every action and aspect of your company is transparent. Even the events that get shredded can be partially reconstructed. Every action is marketing and media. Everything that is transparent can be defined as marketing, an outward expression of your business.

Although you may need to stretch your mind beyond what you learned and now practice, rethink the role of marketing in your organization. See marketing as a strategic line running through every company interaction as a golden thread. This thread runs through every audience (employees, shareholders, suppliers, buyers, press and more) at the quantum speed of the Internet.

If you want to prosper, honor every hand that touches this golden thread – these are your marketing touch points. If you want to grow market share, make sure your product or service creates value for its users. If you want to attract more business and top talent, use the carrot rather than the stick. Do right.

Inspire Your Team

Play to Win

Are you rewarding your team for outrageous thinking about your product or service mix? Do you give them ample room to experiment and defy expectations about such things as new customer experiences, new business models, new strategies, growth ideas, and new lines of revenue? Can they play and not be punished for generating new thinking about old problems? Can they learn by doing?

Or, are you paralyzing them from innovating? Are you punishing them for not following a rigid set of overly managed expectations?

While certain roles depend upon pinpoint accuracy (surgeons, logistics, pharmacy), most industries can be rethought and create more value – and most experiences can be made better – with a sense of wonder and human-centric user viewpoint. Giving your team the freedom to experiment, to play, requires a creative approach to providing experiences. Even serious matters, such as healthcare, can get better results if they experiment.

For example, take Doug Dietz, the Principal Designer for GE Healthcare. For 20 years, Doug designed MRI and CT machines, and then he took a Design Thinking course. He experimented and went into the user experience of his creations instead of just focusing on just the creation itself.

What he realized was that children were terrified by being alone in these cold pieces of technology, so much so they required sedation to endure the negative experience. Without formal orders or a budget, he put together a team of people who cared (including doctors, staff from a children's museum, kids, and families) and had them experiment, or play. They risked failure trying to make a better experience.

The result? With just paint, lights and a little whimsy, the scan rooms turned into adventure portals: an ocean theme in one room where the scanner is a submarine, in another the scanner becomes a tent in a camping experience.

These adventure rooms are wildly successful, inexpensive to executive, and the kids, in the main, no longer require sedation.

Doug is a hero in his company, in the medical industry, and to kids and their families. Something wasn't right—and he risked failure and played, co-created with actual customers—and he found a way to craft a better experience.

Sales went up, too. Play to win. Allow play at your place of business.

Purposeful Innovations

While practical and theoretical strategies and tactics to help companies better innovate can serve as a guide to creating breakthrough and incremental innovations at your firm, they tend to have a higher rate of success in corporate cultures that provide the process, rewards, metrics, training, and resources to innovate. More important, perhaps, is a mindset that fine-tunes the organization. This mindset can galvanize a culture. This mindset is based in an overarching purpose.

There are actions a company can take to awaken purpose so you can harness the natural unlimited resource of human creativity to discover attainable growth through a real innovation program. Here is how purpose generates innovation after value-generating innovation.

First, demonstrate your foremost purpose and vision. Businesses that share their founding dream create possibility.

Founders are leaders who are on fire and who set the expectations that their colleagues should be resonant, relevant, and creative. This purpose and poise should shake people out of the narrow confines of silos and invite people to create a legacy that will outlive them and deliver real value in multiple ways.

Second, innovations should add value to human life, while also enriching the health and well-being of society. Otherwise, what's the point? If the creators are not inspired, then the market will not be. This value should be rooted in your purpose.

Third, give freedom to explore and fail, as part of the mission, which seeks to flesh out the purpose. A business built on trust, rather than fear and stress, will have impassioned team members who show commitment and take responsibility. Giving your team the freedom to make mistakes and learn from them will help inspire them each day and remind them what brought them to the business in the first place.

The opportunity to thrive in a healthy culture of innovation, to be a part of something bigger than themselves, to make a difference, to create a purposeful life while earning a living will bring many happy, profitable returns.

The Role of Play in Innovation

In the Creative Economy, inspiring a sense of play in culture, marketing, and innovation is critical to success. You have to engage your people so that they can engage prospects and customers with a lively sense of mission and purpose. Too often the roles we assign diminish this sense of play.

In a tightly wound corporate culture, business people can become stuck in the role they are forced to assume while at work. They are not allowed to be human and expressive. Like a mask they cannot take off, they turn into a predictable cliché with a limited set of expressions to new ideas.

Talking about breakthrough innovations with such automatons can be as odd as talking to the tax man about poetry, even though innovation could supercharge their careers and help their companies gain or regain a leadership position in a market category. These corporate zombies have lost their sense of play, which is crucial for innovation.

The issue we are really discussing is one of harnessing the most creative value out of your team. As a leader or manager you cannot set up the metrics and measurements and stranglehold the results out of your team. Instead, you have to foster a deeply playful culture that inspires an environment of breakthrough thinking. The best way to cultivate such a culture is to allow play to serve as a North Star of all endeavors.

Let's apply a lesson from a successful author, James Michener, from his autobiography:

> The master in the art of living makes little distinction between his work and his play, his labor and his leisure, his mind and his body, his information and his recreation, his love and his religion. He hardly knows which is which. He simply pursues his vision of excellence at whatever he does, leaving others to decide whether he is working or playing. To him, he's always doing both.

We are not suggesting anything ridiculous here, but something cunningly pragmatic. Companies that blur the line between play and work thrive in the creative economy. Before you bring in a sandbox the size of a swimming pool, realize that we are recommending just a few simple exercises.

What we are saying is your culture needs to formalize a little playtime where the lines of work/play blur. Those responsible for innovation at your place of work should schedule a weekly exercise to expand the capacity to imagine and allow for wild possibilities of team members – one hour per week spent socializing the boon of the human imagination without judgment.

Further, we recommend that every new product development process have at least two formal points in the process where generative, creative thinking without boundaries is encouraged.

Very often, the most effective and brilliant idea sits close to the most ridiculous one, out on a limb next to the fruit and flowers. This idea will only present itself to those who blur the lines, enjoy themselves, and have a mindset that scans for possibility after possibility.

In the end, innovations will be judged by revenue or cost savings – and this counting itself is a deep form of play for the mathematically minded.

Looking for Lightening When Hiring

We've been interviewing a lot lately, trying to fill key positions at the Southern Growth Studio. We have been inundated with well-qualified people seeking exile from soul-crushing corporate cultures and large, global consultancies where they feel like a machine part.

Neither the traditional corporate culture nor the consultant groups that serve them allow these highly talented, often brilliant and always professional individuals to reach their potential in their constricting environments. These relics of the Industrial Revolution hold onto the practices of an era that dehumanized its workforce while stripping the planet of its core resources.

The effect of the rise of corporations has been depicted in books, plays, movies, and television shows: Upton Sinclair, Willy Loman in "Death of a Salesman," "Glengarry Glen Ross" and J.R. Ewing from "Dallas," to name a few. In this paradigm, profit is king and must be attained at all costs. The real costs are more damaging: the soul-crushing demands of conformity to a culture's ethos, language, habits, and defaults for the masses in the system. Thankfully entrepreneurs have been bucking this trend and creating new ways of being a community of work that benefits all involved.

There is an irrepressible, indomitable spirit in such brave people. They cannot help but be themselves. When such people hit a ceiling at work, they respond pragmatically. They make an offer for the situation to change. If it doesn't adapt, they hunt higher ground. These types of leaders create new workspaces and cultures that rectify what kept them and others from hitting their potential in previous settings.

Think about the Googleplex, Herman Miller and any of the other office lifestyle stories. Think about it this way; you can hire someone for a job, a career or a vocation. If you hire someone to do a job, what you see is what you get. They perform a duty for the money with no commitment to the outcome of the success of your venture. If you hire a careerist, you'll bring on an innately political being who embodies the sicknesses of the Industrial

Era's corporate mindset.

If you bring on someone with a sense of mission, a sense of calling, who wants to bring their whole self into a larger context for the good of all parties involved, you strike gold. Such individuals see the world as a place they can make better and see your business as a vehicle for this driving passion. They inspire others – clients and other employees. They remind others why they got into this particular business in the first place.

How do you tell the three types apart? Listen for cues. If someone's main questions hover around money, vacation policy, parking spaces and processes, it's a jobber. If the questions center on org charts, responsibilities, and how decisions are made, you have a ladder climber. But occasionally someone comes in, takes a deep breath and asks systemic questions about why you are in business, how it helps customers, and what can be done to make it better.

Such people have a glint in their eyes, as if they have been struck by lightning, which says it all: drive, intelligence, a sense of collaboration, an inspired work ethic. When hiring, look for the lightning.

Perfect Harmony:
MBA and MFA Mindsets

Business needs to bridge two universes together: the scientific process taught in schools that offer a Master of Business Administration degree and the creative process taught in Master of Fine Arts degree programs.

Reason and intuition feeding each other so that humans can have a better existence—and after all, isn't that why companies should exist?

Right now, we live in a second Age of Reason, fueled with data, analytics, and complex models of information sets that require technical wizardry to slice, dice, and analyze. So many decisions get made with the assurance of such data sets that making a choice without substantial quantitative testing seems absurd and unprofessional. The default paradigm: data, big data, and bigger data.

The Holy Grail of the Industrial Age is something you can manage so much that it can be completely optimized.

However, such a view does not lead or create real, shape-shifting change. More and more data points out problems that cannot be solved without a holistic reassessment of the nature of the problem itself.

Reason alone—the MBA tool set—can diagnose the issue, but not discover new ways to solve it, to radically recreate a company's business model for real innovation

To get more in balance, some smart companies are employing such techniques as Design Thinking and bringing in MFAs to shake up the MBA-industrial revolution-management paradigm.

Here are some tool sets and frameworks that MFAs bring to the table, to help re-humanize work and business:

Wayfinding - MFAs are great explorers and discoverers. They leave the office and the spreadsheet and head into the world for inspiration and to connect with customers in native environments.

Workshop mentality - They do not think of the world as a perfected PowerPoint presentation, backed by numbers. Instead, all projects are a work-in-progress that can be changed, made better, and open to feedback, making the process more collaborative.

Comfortable with uncertainty - MFAs are used to the darkness before the dawn and trust that the answers will come as part of the creative process. Life and business are uncertain, and you need scouts who can stay centered and not get anxious during such times.

Rooted imagination - What sets winning products and services apart is how well the human imagination has been rooted in a particular problem. After working as an artist for some time, this mindset can be a valuable muscle to companies trying to grow market share with new products or by entering new markets.

Empathy - MFAs go into the field, listen to the wants and needs of real people, and gain a critical contextual awareness of the people for whom they are designing products and services.

By offsetting the second Age of Reason with the humanizing skills of the MFA, we can enter a new era of human-centric living. Smart companies are catching on. The others will go the way of the dinosaur.

Parts or Whole?

What do you call a single cell in a huge body, acting counter to the general flow of a body? A rebel cell. The theory of cancer is happening at the corpuses of businesses everywhere. When parts are running in different directions than the whole, there is a schism a hand.

We've used Marcus Aurelius' line already in this book, but it's worth noting again: What is good for the bee is good for the hive. The parts and the whole need to be in harmony, and every part (each initiative, every project, every action or inaction) should play an integral, strategic role. If parts are not working in concert, then efforts and resources are wasted.

How well do your parts sync up to a whole? Does every assignment, every project, every mission add value to the total vision?

Given the buzzword of "corporate waste" or the thousands of killed projects we have seen sitting in a warehouse that's next to a warehouse that's next to a warehouse filled with shelved projects, we think there is a lack of cohesive vision at many companies.

The reason is simple, a lack of vision and leadership. These firms are not applying systems thinking and considering how the parts add or subtract from the whole.

Often, to ignite new growth, we are called into a skunkworks for new product or new market innovation. What we discover, time and time again, is that there are so many parts running in different directions that no one knows what the whole is anymore. This lack of a holistic approach shows that short-sighted, knee-jerk relationships with growth do not work for more than a season and the long-term fallout confuses the whole enterprise.

The corpus is sick without a whole vision. If a company chooses parts as a default—without envisioning how each part adds value to the enterprise—it displays a lack of a coherent vision.

Before a project kicks off, ask how it is related to other projects. Ask if there is a clear path to value. Ask how this part plays into the whole. If you cannot answer, take it to your leaders and demand clarity.

Growing Together — Synthetic Teamwork

In Henry Mintzberg's 1994 landmark book, *The Rise and Fall of Strategic Planning*, the author calls for a new method to create effective strategies. He notes that, "Strategic planning isn't strategic thinking. One is analysis, the other is synthesis."

Mintzberg draws a definitive line between those that create strategy and those that devise the plan, arguing that the two are disparate exercises. He says, "Real strategic change requires inventing new categories, not rearranging old ones," sage wisdom from the '90s that has perhaps been forgotten by many American companies who play defense rather than offense during the economic downturn.

In regards to the nature, nurturing, and definition of innovation, the proverbial pendulum may have swung too far toward the creativity pole and away from quantitative analysis in some ways, causing many to doubt the credibility of innovation as a discipline.

But what if we merged the practices of strategic planning and innovation? Ultimately they seek the same end but each lack skills the other practice possesses. Numbers cannot possibility tell the whole story. Conversely, ideas are a dime a dozen until they are sized and validated.

It is simple really: creativity *plus* analysis equals breakthrough strategy. We believe that if the best of the two practices are brought together, companies can achieve synthetic thinking – one of the highest human functions. Thinking synthetically is the essence of growth – and a guiding principal for a growth team after the strategy is discerned.

The ability to generate original ideas and then validate, organize and monetize them is the holy grail of strategy. Being able to adapt is key. This new growth team then must remain nimble, always observing and testing the market. Strategy is by definition a plan. However, it is a living organism, not a document that is updated every few years and then returned to its dusty shelf.

This new team should be tasked with observing the emerging trends in the world, the socio-economic factors at work and the psychodynamics and drivers behind the groups of people in the value chain. Relying solely on historical data and trends to inform your next move does not generate big leaps in the marketplace.

How do you build this team at your company? Scratch your innovation group. Kill your strategic planning group. Then, repurpose them to a diverse cross-functional team of people tasked with identifying growth opportunities for the company.

This team should not be a homogenous group, forget the common pedigrees. Get some financial guys in there, consumer insights folks, marketing analysts, and don't forget operations. What do they all have in common? Curiosity. Let them explore the possibilities together and then devise the strategy. Then, focus on growth as if the company's life depended upon it, because it does.

The Power of Unplugging

A favorite vacation spot is the Forgotten Coast, a cape wedged in between the sea and a bay. The best part of the location is that a smartphone connection does not work. All of the incessant demands of running a business, having clients, making social media updates, keeping up with news for organizations for whom we serve on boards: poof, gone.

And, when on vacation, no news is the best news of all. By going fallow from the routine, energy renews perspective.

The modern etymological connotation of vacation comes from the 14th century: "freedom from obligations, leisure, release" (from some activity or occupation), from Old French *vacacion* "vacancy, vacant position" (14c.), and directly from Latin *vacationem* (nominative vacatio) "leisure, freedom, exemption, a being free from duty, immunity earned by service," noun of state from past participle stem of vacare "be empty, free, or at leisure." The Latin past participle says it best, "be empty, free, or at leisure."

Only by letting the mind empty out its agendas, notions, biases, mental models, conceptions, and fixed files can new ideas and connections present themselves. This is the power of unplugging—and we, as a culture, may not be unplugging enough to, as our Buddhist friends say, "empty the bowl" or see life and work with a "beginner's mind."

"You can say that taking a holiday is a little bit like going back to childhood, when the world was full of wonder and everything you saw was full of things that you hadn't expected or seen before, you had to calibrate it in your brain," explains Michael M. Merzenich, chief scientific officer of Posit Science. As people age, less and less attention is paid to details in the world. Therefore, keeping a childlike attitude is important — it's one of the reasons children learn so much, he adds. "It's really important that we be challenged about that every so often, that we're reminded to pay attention, that we're really engaged again," Merzenich said.

This implies two key points. Routines can be numbing to our creativity and productivity, and maintaining a fresh perspective reminds us again of the poet Wordsworth's adage "child is the teacher of man." In short hand, vacations allow us to become unstuck and see things anew.

Our advice is to not put off vacation. Take little breaks and practice awareness exercises to see life and work through new eyes as often as possible, too. This way we do not sleepwalk through our work and act like a zombie with an appetite for long lunch breaks at work.

You see, by unplugging the brain begins to notice connections everywhere.

Within a few days, I was taking notes about projects, tearing out magazine articles and highlighting book passages for clients, and thinking of ways to elevate the Studio's creative culture of innovation.

Want to see real opportunity? Unplug for a spell.

Other Innovation Matters

Think Like Nature to Innovate

Nature stores many business success lessons for those smart enough to see them. Companies that prove able to interpret and transfer creation's learnings to its own culture prosper on an on-going basis.

When it comes to pragmatically producing innovations, businesses and people tasked with a new product or service pipeline would do well to take notes from the chrysalis process.

First, note the fragile eggs. If they are not on the right host, in the right environment, they die. These eggs include new incremental ideas, adjacent products or services, and breakthrough business ideas that change the landscape and create a new category and leadership position. At this stage, they all look the same, have a high mortality rate, and need care and support. They are nurtured by white boarding, customer co-creation workshops, and further discovery.

Second, see the larval caterpillar. Eric Caryle's famous children's classic The Hungry Caterpillar provides the right image for this stage. Here the hungry concept grows and eats, and molts and grows, and eats more. This stage of development is where the innovation concept is fed benchmarking studies, modeled out in different sizes, played with in workshops, and where financial cases are drafted. The concept is cared for via the imagination, potential, and excitement. Keep away from internal politics and cocoon the concept with access to a humble, separate budget if the prototypes and preliminary numbers look positive and realistic.

Third, the chrysalis: this is where the magic happens. Just as a Vespa could no more imagine itself transmuting into a Lear jet, the humble concept cannot envision itself taking flight. Here, all cells turn into liquid, totally fluid—do not lose sight of the significance of this metaphor: totally fluid. In this creative, primordial soup, they become the alchemical agent, known to science as "imaginal cells."

These imaginal cells transmute into something much bigger, more beautiful, and with a different nature than the original concept. The process, to extend our overarching analogy, happens when teams come together with a sense of mission and possibility and infuse the concept with radical perspective of what can be.

It is a visionary exercise and those who only criticize or only see limits and hurdles should not be allowed in the room at this stage. They are not fluid enough to learn to fly.

You know the end of the story: the sublime butterfly, new eggs, the process begins again. But, are you creative and smart enough to apply the age-old story to your business?

Can you access your imaginal cells and defy your original nature? Can your business fly?

Only the brave and the capable and the willing should try.

Danger, the Early Warning Sign of Opportunity

Without relying on the predictable places to hide—spread sheets, business buzzwords, risk mitigation plans, past glories—look me in the eyes. Now, point out the potential dangers for your business. When you stutter or express worry about your employees, I will know you're being real, vulnerable, human.

I understand. You *had* a formula that worked. You grew an amazing 10% or more for 12 consecutive years, even if your growth is now declining, or flat, or worse. The market is dynamic. Competitors arise out of nowhere. Customers change habits, brands, or both. Your once magic formula seems commonplace.

The very things that made you different—how you went to market, a product breakthrough—limit your ability to thrive in the new world of today. Perhaps regulations are changing, or import or export laws make it harder to move swiftly.

The world has been moving at the pace of the market for more than a decade, but you've stayed still. Everything has changed, except your company. OK, you may have made an incremental improvement in execution. Here's a consolation prize.

New brands have been born. New business models have entered the market. Service means something else than it did when you started to gain traction. Old customers have not been loyal in the long run. Be real. Back to danger.

Your dangers may save you. They can instruct your next move. An informed and intelligent response to danger, rather than a knee-jerk reply to it, can force a company to make changes that will empower it to thrive—but the firm must be willing to change and capable of being honest with itself.

Woe be on those companies whose pride will not let them adapt, change, and reinvent themselves. Companies so vain as to not change their story and their culture if they are losing market share deserve to live in an isolated, airless bubble.

Wake up—it's dangerous out there—and that's the good news.

The Chinese ideogram for danger also means opportunity. This is not to suggest that we seek out danger, but that we look for openings: broken brand experiences, a chance to wildly redesign service expectations, or outdated business models to reinvent or revise.

Noticing danger means you notice opportunity. Noticing the new connections in the cracks of an older system produces insights about what you can do to reset market expectations by redefining what the category means to customers.

When you are ready to reinvent your business or take a leap into a new market, notice the dangers first. That is where opportunity will be hiding.

You Should Play to Win in Business

At an event in my hometown, A.G. Lafley, CEO of Procter & Gamble, the keynote speaker at the FedEx Institute of Technology's Innovation Expo, shared a wealth of insights on leadership and strategy from his experience and his collaboration with Peter Drucker. However, his most impactful message was so simple, many in the audience may have missed it — strategy is about making choices. That's all there is to it. Make decisions about what business you are in and how you win in this business, then stick to them.

We've found that making definitive choices is difficult for many businesses. They prefer to keep their options open and not limit themselves to a particular market, customer, or value proposition. This is largely fear based: the fear of change, the fear of being wrong, and the fear of losing it all. Sometimes there is too much noise, too many things to consider and leaders become paralyzed because the path forward isn't clear. Not making committed decisions about the strategy is far worse for the health of the business. The world is dynamic, it is changing and yet the company is static.

Lafley attributes much of his success at P&G to the choices he has made. Many of these choices were not popular, like when he sold Jif peanut butter, a profitable business unit. It's certainly not easy to let go of a cash flowing legacy business. Especially with incoming calls from past leaders and board members questioning this decision. Lafley was able to triple the company's market cap by making the decision to grow P&G's core, extend into beauty and personal care, and expand into emerging markets. Peanut butter was no longer a strategic fit.

He will tell you that the purpose of strategy is to win. Lots of companies are playing without the intent to win. Just being on the field isn't good enough. To win you must clearly define winning. Winning companies have a unique position in their industry, a sustainable advantage, and deliver a superior value versus the competition.

Lafley points out in his book that a potentially winning strategy shortens your odds, it does not guarantee success. Nothing in life is certain. Do the analysis to minimize risk and give yourself a decision advantage. Then make the decision.

People think that innovation is about wildly creative ideas that break the mold – and it is to a certain extent. But it really is just solid execution within smart strategy. Lafley is well known for turning P&G into an organization that innovates quickly to delight its customers. How did he do this? With discipline, fortitude and action. He's laser focused on where to play and how to win.

Why Limit Yourself?

When consulting with clients in this Memphis area, we often have to deliver the bad news first. This bitter pill usually comes in the form of a Sunset Analysis that details when the client's once market-leading products will be costing more to keep in production than generating revenue.

Outside of the region, we do not see this problem as widespread. There is a sin of hope being applied here again and again, as if one day history will revert and a company's flagship product will suddenly regain the sales and stature it once had when it was relevant, innovative, and competition was limited. This type of thinking depresses the region and drains your company of its ability to thrive.

Moreover, when a company sees the statistically modeled point at which they start burning cash it is a telling moment. Either they accept the facts or they don't. Most often they enter a four-phase process of accepting death and decline. They try and argue, make excuses, and then realize that they must change or die.

The change itself serves as a mirror of the organization's psyche. Too often a company facing a sunset of a major product line will force a me-too product in the market because it seems like easy pickings. There is already proven demand for the product line and we have a product line that makes sense to add this one to it, thanks to distribution. This knee-jerk approach floods the market with junk and makes a market segment into a commodity war.

A few, brave companies take such news as a personal challenge to reinvent themselves, their product lines, and the market they serve. These rare birds dare to fly higher, take calculated risks, expect some experimentation in the process, and don't rush into playing copycat.

Instead of noticing what they can steal and adapt from the completion, they notice the gaps in the market that competitors do not offer. They notice trends in adjacent industries. They work with consumers to figure out the unmet need that may create a transformational opportunity in the market that will propel their growth.

We all get feedback every day. What separates winners from losers is their ability to creatively respond to every point of feedback and the ability to see opportunity instead of fear. The mindset of an organization makes all the difference.

The question is: why limit yourself? There are several mid-market companies in the region who define themselves as manufacturers. In reality, they are branded product companies. If they choose they could compete with global companies such as L'Oreal, Proctor & Gamble, and others. Instead, they choose to make passable products and place them on low-end store shelves even though they are losing market share rapidly.

How are you going to respond? We say let's grow.

Consumers Driving
Healthcare Innovation

Everyone in the U.S. complains about healthcare—the rising costs of insurance premiums and co-pays, the lack of innovation, the poor experience at doctor's offices and hospitals, and price of medications.

The landscape of big healthcare is eroding faster than the biggest players can adapt.

Thanks to malpractice, the Internet, the rise of specialists and decline of general practitioners, integration with complementary and alternative medicine, and other factors—consumers feel as if they must drive their own healthcare.

Gone are the days when actions are blindly followed, as in "the doctor told me to take this _____ and do _____."

Instead, Internet research leads to second-guessing and attempts at self-diagnoses, mass cyberchondria. Both scenarios lead to information anxiety. Too little and too much unfiltered information causes this quiet despair. The emerging paradigm finds consumers lost, bewildered, looking for sources and solutions that help make health care make sense for them—and willing to switch to what works for them.

This tension creates a gap of opportunity for disruptive entrants into the market. With $2.8 trillion at play, everyone will race to get their piece of the pie, from well-established companies outside of healthcare, to service providers offering new models of care, to start ups. Hopefully, healthcare companies will recognize the need to transform their business model and their product and service mix, or risk dying on the vine.

A recently released study by the Health Research Institute (HRI) called "Healthcare's New Entrants: Who will be the industry's Amazon.com" makes plain the threat to the established players:

Revenue will circulate differently, and to many new players. Consumers, spending more of their own money, are exerting greater influence and going beyond the traditional industry to find what they want and need. In the New Health Economy, purchasers increasingly will reward organizations providing the best value, whether it's an academic medical center, a tech company with a great app, or a healthcare shopping network.

Traditional providers have not yet caught the tide of change, nor have they figured out how to diversify their revenue streams. A single innovation can put a huge dent in the market. For example, if half of all U.S. patients opted to administer an at-home strep test, it could hurt the traditional provider network as much as $68 billion. This move would benefit consumers, the company that makes the test, and the retailer, but is a seismic shift for doctor office revenues.

Huge players are scrambling to make an impact: Walgreen's, Google, Time Warner, Target, as well as an increasing number of healthcare technology start ups.

Who will win? The ones who listen to consumers, as they are the driving force of the change.

Entrepreneurial Urge to Innovate

Zero Budget — What a Boon

Entrepreneurs come alive when all odds are stacked against them. Think of the famous stories. Walt Disney and Frank Lloyd Wright going bankrupt several times until their visions pay off. Edison brokering the GE deal that meant the West would use the type of electricity the wizard of Menlo Park created. Steve Jobs kicked out of Apple, starting Next. The old saying holds true: the darkest hour is just before the dawn.

Most corporate drones lack this fortitude — and one reason is that it is impossible to take risks if you have the comfort of knowing you have a budget. Not until a concept stares into the void — of life, of death — does it earn the right to try and thrive in the market.

Nothing stymies innovative thinking more than the inability to conceptualize a pipeline of products, services, and leaps in business models without relying on a budget.

Once a budget is provided, it typically narrows the scope of thinking. Worse than constricting the vision and possibilities, budgetary thinking keeps lazy professionals in a rut. Acting in default mental models, they will compare what they do now, how they do it, and what they are trying to change by thinking about the how the budget is used today. In essence, the actions inherent in the budgetary mindset pre-set the limits and actions of planning. The golden handcuff theory applies to new product and service concepts when conceived with the constraints of a budget as much as it does to professionals stuck in a bad situation because of a financial compromise.

One exercise that taps innovative thinking is to imagine that you have no money to birth and socialize a new concept, idea, service, or product. As a pilot study, give two teams an assignment. Have them develop a breakthrough concept that will increase top-line revenue by 10 percent or more within 18 months. Then tell both groups that they have to get internal buy-in, develop a go-to-market plan and campaign, and craft a full marketing strategy.

Next, tell the first group that they have a budget of $2 million. The second group will have to move ahead without any internal funding. Give them a day to craft and workshop draft plans. Then, it is presentation time.

What you might discover is that the group without the budget is forced to find new and inventive ways to connect with buyers and influencers — and that the radical thinking they employ can be adapted to other, more mature lines of business.

Money can be as much of a numbing drug as it can be an active current; it depends on how it is used. By role-playing and acting as if there is no budget, those in charge of an innovation are forced to think outside of their normal habitual patterns and limited experiences.

Force your team to get outside of its comfort zone. Assign a zero-budget exercise. You may be amazed at how cunning, crafty, and creative your team can be when forced to imagine the impossible.

Status Quo: The Big Lie

There's a big deceit looming over the global marketplace, perhaps the most prevalent and insidious bias in business. This big lie is that the status quo exists. Nothing stays the same. Companies who strive to keep things the way the presently are—one definition of status quo—live a lie that is not sustainable. They get fixed and rigid, locked into a certain way of counting on the world, and then they crumble and fall.

In a dynamic marketplace, the current state of affairs never becomes fixed. As the housing bust reminded us, you can never bet on the market acting and reacting the same way for too long. Likewise, look at Kodak. The giant waited too long, hoping against hope that the market might, for an unimaginable reason, revert to an outmoded technology. The refusal to accept reality and the insistence on keeping the status quo allowed new era companies like Microsoft and Google to bid on Kodak's only relevant assets at bargain basement bankrupt prices. We could list tragedy after tragedy, case after case. The sickness is the same: the big lie.

The key to this column is ensuring your business or place of employment does not allow itself to hide in the shadows of the status quo. Good is never good enough, really, when you can do something great. So, put safeguards in place. Challenge your co-workers, your employees, each other to identify when entropy sets in. Also, know that the status quo can cost you a lot of money. So many forms of business operations have become more effective and more cost-effective. Why settle for a tired routine when it isn't working for you at the highest return?

Proactivity drives away the big lie—and is less expensive than remedial actions. It takes enterprise-strength and a hefty budget for Change Management to fix an entrenched issue remedially. Proactivity cures the parts of the corpus that are drifting on autopilot.

Acting as if the status quo were real may limit growth significantly. In a rigid culture, a lack of attunement to what drives the business means that no one will have eyes to see, or the heart to seize opportunities. Here, a paralyzing resistance to change means that no one is inspired to think about new forms of top-line growth.

The big lie damages your brand. Branding is a game of building momentum and creating a shorthand out of a name. If your brand is known for being inflexible, rigid, and status quo-driven, we hope you work in the security industry where such traits may be seen on the positive side of the ledger. Otherwise, you will never gain the type of equity that amounts to a respectable valuation.

Most important, status quo thinking keeps you at risk of becoming obsolete in the market. As the farmer says, "If you're not growing, you're dying."

If your business operates under a business model that seems outdated, it probably is. If your company suffers the status quo bias, ask for help. For a business, lapsing into a status quo mindset means lapsing into a harmful delusion that markets stay static. The speed of change increases every moment. While retreating to the status quo may seem like a good defensive strategy, it actually is a worse trap. Beware.

Feed Yourself First

So many new business ventures die on the vine. Statistics vary, and we'll keep the details of the debate to a minimum here. Let's say that one in twenty make it. Let's define the Making It as either having a profitable company after five years of existence or selling to a larger firm for a wealth-creating sum.

We meet a lot of serial entrepreneurs at the Studio. They have grown start up after start up, and sold company after company. We befriend them, soak in their experience and hard-earned wisdom, and take in their stories. Their insights and actions defy most conventional B-school lore. The oral tradition holds true in business. We learn lessons from those who have walked the path before.

The primary lesson: pay yourself first. This is a very simple fact of nature, yet so many companies forget it. If you don't eat, you will not survive. Make no mistake. You will be tested. There will be periods where cash flow will trickle to a mere drop no matter how well you are capitalized. Accounts receivables will be spoken for by bills from the utility company, credit cards, partners, vendors, contractors, IRS, and the list goes on and on and on.

If you stay alive, all of these fine organizations and people will prosper. If you go out of business, declare bankruptcy, and take the downward spiral into shame and hiding, no one wins.

Therefore, the advice of the winners is to feed yourself first. Stay alive. You cannot reach the mission or vision of your company if you starve into oblivion. As the brave hero in Greek Mythology plugged his ear to keep from hearing the sirens' song, plug your ears. Keep the bill collectors at bay until you are in a position to make it right.

Once you reach a cash flow positive position, make it right, and then count the profits. Stay alive. Feed yourself first. It's that simple.

Growth: That Crazy Talk

Call it the entrepreneurial instinct, innovation, business savvy, whatever you want: strategic growth is how business prospers.

While some Mid-South and Memphis-area ventures stand as global luminaries of category-defining growth such as the modern grocery store and overnight delivery, most area businesses cower when facing growth.

Growth is a natural source of power, a wellspring or volcano. Businesses, like nature, live a lifecycle. Organizations are as alive as a person; yet, most businesses do not harness the growth process to gain an advantage.

Rare companies that address growth by a mix of planning and making well-timed, well-orchestrated adaptions to their plan make positive headlines.

In most cases, dynamics change market conditions and businesses retrench. They do more of what no longer works with increased vigor and focus. They react in fear. These actions dig a grave.

More than ever, every business needs to find, discover, and implement fresh, rewarding ways to procure and retain business. Remain relevant, demonstrate value, and compete with formally unthinkably high levels of service.

At the time when companies need to radically rethink their market strategy, they hide behind walls of denial and the sleepy, sentimental practices that worked in the 70s, 80s or 90s.

Sadly, we witness this reenactment at business after business: "Growth. What do you mean? We're just sitting, waiting for the phone to ring. ... We don't need a plan. ... We just trade customers back and forth with our competition," and on and on. We get thrown out for *crazy talk*.

Excuses and justifications, we've heard them all. They add up to a deafening wake up call for the whole business culture of the Mid-South.

Memphis? Do you really want to become just the world's warehouse? Or, can we retool our business climate and invent new product pipelines and services that create new markets and generate serious returns?

Will the next Abe Plough, Clarence Saunders, Fred Smith, Pitt Hyde, Elvis Presley please stand up?

What will this generation's visionaries look like? What core markets will they disrupt or create? How will they impact the world and infuse the local economy by being a top employer and recruiter for the area? Perhaps it will grow out of your neighborhood?

Let's apply this crazy talk to existing companies. What old-line companies will transform their business model and product/service mix to keep growing? What companies will quicken their demise by not changing?

These are crazy times. Listen to the crazy talk.

What keeps you sane: accept the fact that growth is a reality in business. What keeps you inspired is when you see your topline revenue growing because you guided change in your favor. You have a strategy. You adapt. You keep the firm in the present moment, instead of living a tired dream and repeating outmoded practices.

Will the next company ready to grow, stand up. Memphis needs you. The world needs you.

In this article we will explore growth, innovation, and entrepreneurial issues and profile real, Mid-South examples. We want to give voice to strategic growth in the Memphis area. We invite you to help create a thriving business culture. Talk that crazy talk. Wherever you are, action wins. Dream. Measure. Do.

Stuck in a Rut? Meet Dis- and Re-

Perspective is everything. In life and work-life, this adage proves true time and time again.

If you can see opportunity without pre-set lenses, you are more prone to make advantageous use of this gift. If you harness the skill to zoom out and zoom in, you see your business in many different settings, in different categories and segments, and serving different customers. We, at the Studio, cannot empathize the power of fresh thinking and the cleansing of a cached perspective.

Let's look at the opposite skill. Your organization has attained the glory of management, operational excellence. You have orchestrated the entire flow of work down to a predictable algorithm.

While you may realize a short-term bump in cost-savings because you have optimized efficiencies, something is not right. No matter how tightly you put the screws to your sales team, sales are down, heading toward flat. What you manufacture is no longer desired at a premium price. Imports are killing your once sacred margin. The market has changed. Distributors turn your loyal relationship into a parts-dealer relationship. Low cost is king. And, they will not take your higher margin products to their clients. The market has changed. Your business model, although optimized, is no longer viable. You have gotten so rigid in your perspective that you cannot adapt and transform the business to meet today's demands. You have essentially created a trap, built upon the faulty assumption that your snapshot of reality from which you derived the operational algorithm was an eternal truth.

Now, you must change or face extinction. If you kept a fresh perspective—and the ability to zoom in and zoom out—you would have never found yourself in such a costly bind.

Leaders today realize that they need to disorient their perspectives and reorient themselves to the market with fresh eyes on a daily or weekly basis to avoid getting stuck in such a deep rut. The market is never linear; nor should businesses be.

There are exercises leadership teams can do to disorient their perspectives, think creatively about their businesses, and awaken to a broader sense of opportunities for their firms.

If you are stuck, and what once worked well is working against you, try some creative disorientation and role-playing to way find and lead a way out.

Private Label Becomes the Branded Product

Almost everyday the Studio faces challenges that private label competitors impose upon our branded products clients. More and more private label brands are taking lessons out of the innovation and brand strategy playbooks and getting ahead of the once category-leading brand product.

Advances in product development, consumer empathy ethnographies, innovation, packaging, manufacturing, and branding—not to mention owning the point-of-sale in the retail stores—give the once me-too product knock offs about to soar above the leading consumer goods companies and, again, beat them at their own game.

Look at the redesigned Target or Walgreens or Kroger brands, for example. They have the ideal mix: right product, right price, right place, and right packaging and experience.

Private labelers have become the brand of choice, the default brand in non-commoditized categories.

Moreover, these brands are hiring global thought leaders from brand and innovation firms and creating new products that give them the competitive edge. You can call this move the offensive strategy of private labeling.

The defensive strategy still works well, too. Take an example from the Body Wash category. Two leading companies come up with competing products. One is black and the other is red. By the time they hit the shelf, the private labelers have reserve engineered the product with some verisimilitude, and now they too offer a black and a red product. The difference is the branded product costs 10-times as much as the steeply discounted private-label product.

Private label was once only a defensive game, a copy-and-cost-cut play. Now, however, private labelers are creating new brands and products that raise them up the value chain with an increasing focus on higher quality, better experiences, and their companion, a higher-shelf price point.

Private label already won the price war and continues to turn categories into commodities. Now, private labelers are beginning to win the brand wars.

Given this situation, it is time from branded product companies to activate new business models: create joint ventures, develop radical and ownable new products, sell in new channels, or launch their own stores.

Keys for Compelling Storytelling

Most innovations fail because they are too good, too smart, and too unfamiliar to the existing business to risk launching. The last phase of a full-cycle innovation process – storytelling – was rushed. A PowerPoint deck was created using the language of the business culture, unconsciously framing the new concept in the old world of the doldrums of existing operations. The new ideas get applause for their "brave, fresh thinking." then are summarily placed on the back burner to be ignored for eternity.

A little savvy storytelling could have salvaged the innovation, helped launch it in the market, and fueled the company's top-line growth. Here are a few keys to successful storytelling at this critical stage gate.

Know your audience. At this point your audience includes those whose bonuses are tied to short-term results. So if you propose a long-term disruption, make sure you have interim, short-term steps that will see a fast bump in revenue. Or, if you have a range of solutions, think through their concerns and offer a portfolio of quick wins and longer-term risker, but higher value solutions. Also, if your fieldwork with consumers or customers yielded new insights about the brand and its elasticity than reams of traditional market research data, this human-centric approach can reframe their perspectives of the market. This is high-value primary research.

Do two things at once. If you can discuss how solving real issues for people while solving a vexing business problem, it's an epic win-win. Weave these two threads together in a way that demonstrates a deep learning and a shape-shifting opportunity.

Two worlds at once. You are presenting to business people. Use the language of business. At this stage you should have done your homework. Model out the market size. Understand what competitors offer. Have a detailed business case and preliminary pro forma prepared. Know costs and price strategy. But also, pepper your numbers with the quicksilver of potential, the poetics of new possibility. Explain how this irrefutable plan not only takes competitive market share, but also grows previously unmapped territory for the brand and company, new headroom.

All good stories take listeners on a journey of discovery. Something surprising, insightful, delightful arises in the course of the tale. Ultimately, everyone who hears it should view the world and their place differently after hearing a well-told, compelling story.

If it is your job to get approval on a product or service innovation, master these keys or you will end up on the unnamed, dusty shelves of forgotten history.

(Lack of) Innovation at Non-Profits

Through the Southern Growth Studio, I have the great honor to work with non-profits. Big ones. Growing ones. And ones on the verge of collapse. There is an odd tendency for almost all of these organizations to respond to innovations in the same way; they desire them deeply but are wildly timid. It's a dizzying and paralyzing fear-based response. *What if it doesn't work? I don't know ...* They yearn to roll out a new program or recreate an experience that gets better results, but something nagging in the culture keeps them from enacting the very thing that may set them apart and catalyze their potential.

Fear-based thinking keeps many non-profits from making sustainable growth leaps and assuming a stable leadership position. Yet, driven professionals long for holistic, positive change in branding, marketing, operations, programs, and the experience they offer donors to meet their noble missions. Short-term fear of the wrath of internal politics keeps the best and brightest from creating long-term gains. Real innovation cannot take root in such cultures.

Instead, employees covet the famous, albeit rare, examples of bravery in the non-profit space and zealously want their own me-too versions of these iconic initiatives. You hear again, again, and yet again: "what is our pink ribbon?" and "what is our ice bucket challenge?" While these stand as good examples of branding and marketing, they do not classify as a breakthrough innovation. Innovation—rethinking a business model, an experience, and a service—is even rarer at such culture.

The answer: do the work. There is a program, an unforgettable icon, a new experience, an innovation never known in the non-profit world that is yours for the taking, but you have to invest the time, resources, and care to cultivate it.

More critical to its success, you have to prepare your culture to embrace new thinking and calculated risks. You cannot reap the benefits of brave thinking and successful execution of something new to the industry if you do not craft the culture that embraces such thinking. Ultimately, it is the curse of the incremental improvement—symptomatic of culture that have too much middle management and not enough real leadership in place.

The sad fact is that innovation methods could be the most cost-effective tools for helping a non-profit to meet its mission. As well, it could discover donor-centric insights on deeper engagement that could transform a giving cycle from a transactional-based annual gift into an inspired relationship where donors become the core evangelists and most avid fundraisers throughout the year.

I'd love to learn about non-profits benefiting from Innovation practices—and encourage readers to send me case studies.

The world needs these non-profits to prosper, instead of suffering a me-too ADD where it wants to copy the Next Big Thing without doing the actual work of stimulating, cultivating, and launching innovative programs.

Don't Make a Shrine of Your Success

Remember the scene in the black and white section of the Wizard of Oz when one of the farmers (who later transforms into the Tin Man) tells Auntie Mae, "They're going to make a statue of me one day!" Her response handled the ego inflation with a dose of pragmatic farm wisdom. As she pointed to his next chore, she retorts, "Don't start posing for it now."

The egotistical position of some brands (products, services, and organizations) that have *made it* put them in a dangerous mindset, a rigid alabaster-like shrine that sets into a predictable formula, loses its growth drive, and becomes an imitation of its once-great self.

Lost are the best attributes: genuine curiosity about the market and customers, an infusion of fresh thinking about every aspect of the business, and real insight on competitors. Gone are the intrinsic brand-propelled moves that once were a palpable force of culture. Now, experiments are shunned as they don't fit into the "core business" or "mission" even if the core business or mission are getting copied by private label, me-too companies, or fast-growing start ups that popped on the scene out of nowhere.

Innocence has been lost. Experiences have reached operation excellence and optimized to a pinnacle, a predictable outcome. It worked like gangbusters until market trends changed. Then, you are a defensive, rigid shrine, ready to be smashed or put in a closet. You've lost your flexibility and native instincts. It's hell—just ask Dante, for whom the Devil was frozen in a lake of ice.

For many of our Innovation clients, they must reframe, and then retool how they make money. What propelled them in the market has been calcified into a safe, robotic set of responses: "this is what we do" and "this is how we do it."

The business matures into a fixed set of overly managed short-term outcomes—and are tied to each individuals metrics and performance-based bonuses. This limits true growth and innovation. A death knell that attracts the timid.

The antidote is to invest—both financially and energetically—in recapturing a fresh, fluid perspective on your core business, culture, business model and getting to know your customers again, as if for the first time. As well, you have to tie longer-term metrics to the innovation pipeline, welcome new business models, and reward insight generation.

The key lesson: don't make a shrine of yourself—and if you do, smash it and start working on the next thing, then the next. Evolve.

The Real Work of Innovation

Being creative. Generating thousands of ideas. Making employees feel heard, valued, more than a cog in a machine. These are the superficial by-products of an in-depth innovation discipline.

Unto themselves, these tiny crumbs of the vast buffet of genuine innovation methods are not an Innovation effort. They represent mere pacification. Any board member or C-Suite executive who believes they have the Innovation boxed checked because they have an online idea submission forum and a committee that ranks ideas needs to resign. Enough with lip service. Stop the confusion of New Product Development and Innovation. You must commit. Otherwise, close down the parade of ideas and quit the charade. Your innovative competitors will buy you when you are on the block.

The real work of innovation is real work. The Studio has had to reframe and then reboot entire innovation efforts at clients after they got a bad taste in their mouth outsourcing whole projects and failing to embrace them - an expensive learning experience.

There is a better way. Instead, embed several team members inside your organization with project-based guides who can help set up An Innovation Framework and Process that works for your culture. Learn processes and methods. Do not stop until you get results—then, you will find no compelling business reason to stop.

Already you have begun developing a culture that embraces Innovation. Otherwise, you will never reach a point of sustainable market leadership.

The same lesson can be applied to service firms and non-profits playing with innovation. To innovate you have to do the work. As the old saying goes, "No one can do your push ups for you." You can hire a coach, but you have to do the work.

The real work of innovation means having your employees working alongside deeply trained experts to build muscle by completing real projects that can dramatically improve top-line growth while signaling that real innovation is part of the fabric of this culture—not just toyed with or outsourced.

Metrics for Front-End Innovation Projects

Anxiety hits middle managers the hardest.

"What are the metrics?"

We get this question all the time from nervous managers, directors, and VPs who are struggling with the philosophical underpinnings of front-end innovation. They are eager to launch an innovation program, but want to be able to foresee the outcome before embarking on a journey of discovery. This is a different game than B-school thinking from the Industrial age, and to prosper here you must be comfortable with some uncertainties on the outset. Hard metrics cannot be realistically assigned until the front-end work has been completed. **Not everything in business or life is a machine of predictability, an algorithm where you input data, access risks, and output gain.**

This is the good news. Front-End Innovation is a different mindset, one of exploration and possibility, that then transforms the potential into actual business strategies, channel plans, and something around which metrics can measure at the end of the cycle.

Don't worry. The metrics will naturally present themselves as part of the process, but we don't know many things right out of the gate. Let's be real, mature, and not acting from a fear-based mindset of perfection before we do empathy work in the field or break open a disruption that may change the course of the industry. You don't want to tie the runner before the race. The following list offers a good representative sample of why adaptive rather than prescribed intelligence need be applied at stage:

• How will the empathy inform the project's starting objectives?

• What do your customers really desire, even without being able to articulate it?

• What is the actual problem for which we are solving and will generate rationing possible solutions?

• How incremental and short-term or disruptive and game changing will the concepts be? Or will a portfolio be a mix of all of these stages?

• What will be the costs of the portfolio of innovations, marketing, and the projected return?

You know if you are asking these types of questions that you are at this precipice, this territory that is not yet mapped for your company, one with vast potential market headroom.

Innovations create new value by listening to the market, not solving a business problem. Metrics are drafted to manage business problems. This stage follows.

"So, may we settle upon something? I mean, we are going to invest a lot of money. What will be the return?"

Can deep learning be the sole metric? Until the Co-creation phase is complete and we can rough out business cases on the concepts that consumers or customers deem most viable?

Warning: Assigning metrics too early in the front end of innovation process would be kill the spirit of invention and deafen the Empathy stage.

Internal Benefits of Practicing Innovation

Ultimately, innovation must be defined by the new value it creates for an organization. Sure, there are many innovations that create nominal value by shaving costs at various points of the value chain. These incremental product or service adaptations are a positive by-product of having an innovation discipline. Sights need to be set higher to really change a category for the better and create a sustainable leadership position in the market.

Other tangible and valuable benefits often get short thrift when metrics are applied and valuations placed on an Innovation Program, most of which are internal. Here are several benefits of fostering an innovation discipline inside your organization, if you are on the fence about adding this discipline or its value.

1. It's the most inexpensive way to **tap employee engagement**. For the cost of a few days of focus, sticky notes, lunch, sharpies, expo markers and whiteboards, you can train an army of innovators inside your organization. During this "bootcamp," you can train with the basic methods of innovation (Lens Smashing, Wicked Thinking, Design Thinking, Opportunity Mapping) to inspire new thinking and a possibility mindset with your team members. This type of training is a potent form of Leadership Development and Collaboration Training. What is this training worth to you? Your best people with have a formal way to take on new challenges, experiment with concepts, invent and test, and be entrepreneurs and problem solvers on your behalf.

2. **Solve a vexing market or customer problem**. For training purposes, you can use an as-yet unsolved problem vexing your venture as the Project Challenge of the workshop. This way you get fresh perspectives, guided via a problem solving methodology, on your Achilles' heel without making it a formal project or hiring a bloated consulting firm to solve it for

you. At the end of the bootcamp, the problem will have been explored deeply, defined better than before, solved hundreds of ways, and co-created with real customers to optimize the value of the experience for them. Yes, in two days, while you are training your people, a double win. How much is solving this problem worth to you?

3. **Retain your talent.** People leave an organization to pursue new ideas, new learning, new opportunities, as well as a sense of making a difference in an organization. Having an Innovation Program would help you retain those who are on the fence, looking over the fence at greener grass. The war for talent has never been greater. By offering growth and nominal investment in employee's ideas, you retain the most ambitious and naturally inspired employees, the high-potential ones. As well, you will end up with a pipeline of prototypes and concepts that could galvanize your business. How much is retaining talent worth?

4. **Collaboration as a team sport.** If your team practices a collaborative process, learn the value of working together to solve a vexing issue; trust gets built. These abilities to collaborate and establish the golden bonds of trust add the highest returns of team productivity. How much are trust and collaboration worth to you?

So, the costs are a few days, some markers, and at worse some travel and testing incentives. For this meager investment, you get repaid with more robust employee engagement, solving of a critical problem, retain your key talent, and let them build real trust and collaboration skills. Other arguments could be that your organization will be more adaptive and more innovative, crafting a culture of high growth. These are just four of the many internal benefits of practicing innovation.

If you add up the top three alone, the value far exceeds the nominal cost. In fact, it just seems like a thick-headed, wrong move not to implement as soon as you finish this column.

Two Kinds of Empathy
for Successful Innovation

If you unpack the stories of most successful innovations, you'll find that a deep immersion into the user experience of a product or service is the key that often unlocks the potential of the concept. Call it ethnography. Call it primary research. Call it field research. Call it empathy.

For more than a decade, getting Research-and Development and Marketing teams to go out into the context of the field has been the missing element in the insights work that drives meaningful innovations.

Getting to know representatives that may use the products or services being innovated and their worldview is such an inherently valuable thing to do—and it's the essence of smart business, the kind that keeps its hand on the pulse of its market.

But, it's not everything.

Now, the pendulum has swung too far in the other direction. Consumer-centric, customer-centric, and user-centric studies often led to a one-dimensional knowing of a complex problem—and if you put too much weight on just this primary data set, you miss other worlds of possibilities and other insights into opportunities.

Esoteric Empathy—let's call it what it is. Getting inside customer (if B2B) or consumer (if B2C) heads in the inner work that mines the psyche for unarticulated needs in the market via their experience. For the sake of clarity, let's call this work Esoteric Empathy, as it discerns often unspoken needs from a relatively small group of people.

Going deep with real people can be really potent for an innovation project, but it cannot answer all the questions that both started the project and also arise in the course of the project. Here, we must call on a different type of knowing to filter and frame the first-person findings. This is market awareness, or Exoteric Empathy.

Using such tools as market sizing, competitive studies, trend data, benchmarking of adjacent industries (and many others) gives a badly needed context for the esoteric empathy.

Wisdom is never original. Innovation is easy—if you work to understand the inner lives of your target customers and the outer forces of the market in which they dwell and you do business. Apply both Esoteric and Exoteric empathy to ensure a successful front end of innovation process.

Three Steps to Keep from Drowning in Big Data

"We have so much data, but no answers." This phrase echoes down the halls of all of the larger clients with whom we meet. In a quantitative world, where there is every dimension of research and analysis available, unreality multiples.

The business world is drowning in data and, by the level of panic and anxiety, lost its rudder.

The ability to have machines figure out existing systems, such as playing chess or optimizing a logistics supply chain, is a great boon to humanity—and it is the role of proper and attentive management. But even the smartest predictive analytics cannot provide answers that move customers or consumers, nor can they re-imagine an industry, nor can they redesign a service experience.

Yet, we expect Big Data to act like Santa Claus with a Calculator, granting us every greedy wish we can conjure and to answer our unexplored and unmet needs as well.

We have entrusted the most ingenious and inventive humanity to a faster processor rather than to a whole-brained mix of human intuition, creativity, tempered with reason and business savvy.

No machine can empathize with clients and prospects. For this obvious reason, human-centric design is the foremost competitive leverage any company can employ. A machine, at the end of the day, will work off the inputs you provide, whereas real people will convey depth, feeling, trust, preference, and imagination.

Big data quantitative modeling has its place at the table, but don't expect any of the "insights" to tell you how to grow, how to innovate, and how to make critical new product decisions.

You can drown in the ocean of big data looking for such answers. These answers will not present themselves fully as the output of a machine.

Therefore, ensure that these steps are part of your overall strategic process:

1. Employ people who know how to interpret data on behalf of your organization. Ideally, a team of number crunchers, marketers, and social scientists should review the trends together. With this mix you can spot the trends, create concepts on how to capitalize on them, and understand some of the factors at hand. Figure out what questions to explore more deeply is the key work at this stage.

2. Talk with consumers (customers in a B-2-B world) about the trends you are discovering. Once you have ferreted out the right questions and have some heuristics indicating a shift in buying patterns and behavior, it is best to talk to real people about the trends and how they are affecting them. Try a mix of consumer empathy intercept interviews, co-creation workshops, and group conversations about the changing landscape. Respect them. Empathize. Not force a point or agenda at this stage.

3. Sketch new concepts, new products, and new experiences. After you break down what the data is implying from various viewpoints and get a real sense of the market, new concepts of products and services can be generated, tested, refined, then measured and brought to the market. This is a human act of creation. Getting user feedback and making adaptive revisions is part of the cycle.

In the wonderful, recursive, messiness of our humanity, there is an unlimited resource of creativity. Tap into it to spark something new to life.

Big data is a great asset, but becomes more valuable when coupled with the messy creative process that has to power to transform people and companies.

Built In Client Obsolesce

Here's a Studio secret. We have a natural client attrition plan inherent in our business model. We not only lead innovation projects, but also give away our practices as part of the process.

When you set up your projects as <u>both</u> a value-generating project and an innovation-training program, it is a great success when clients complete a project cycle and then are eager to take off their training wheels.

They feel ready to tackle the next project challenge on their own, filled with inspiration, a methodology that produces results, and enough authority to have their breakthrough and disruptive concepts accepted by the leadership of their organizations. They have changed their culture, to be more adaptive, value-generating, and customer-centric.

We live for the moment when we have worked with our clients to the point where they have the creative confidence, inner authority, and experience, knowledge, and respect of the processes of innovation to handle projects themselves to a successful finish—a real cause for celebration.

We see this shift as the deepest win. Clients have worked hard, learned to better collaborate, trained, hired internally, and have reached a level of skill where they have embedded the discipline of innovation within their firm's operational model and strategic plan.

It's a tangible milestone of growth—and it's happening with non-profits, business-to-business companies, consumer product companies, durable goods companies, health care and financial services organizations, and fast-growing start ups.

The heart of the secret is this point: by seeding innovation, we help the region regenerate itself with a vast toolset for complex problem solving. We grow the innovation troops, the innovation market, and can use this talent to help the quality of life improve at three key levels: the individual, the organizational, and culture itself.

Real innovation is a gift that keeps giving.

Six Sets of Eyes for Innovation Work

To successfully foster an innovation, you have to look through *at least* six different sets of eyes.

First, you have to unlearn everything you know. Admit it. You are biased, pre-programmed, and your bonus is tied into business results. Apply sincere empathy with people who do not know as much as you.

To enter a beginner's mind and renew how you see the context of the market, you will need to both hang out with "naive consumers" and also look through the eyes of **The Consumer.**

Next, you have to gain the perspective of **The Hunter.** The Hunter's sight scans the horizon for opportunity and acts on instinct to locate its game.

Sense the risks, discern the energies of the culture, understand how decisions are made, find partners, know the inherent biases, and mentally chart out where hurtles and traps may be.

Then, you have to take on the eyes of **The Farmer.** First look at the existing culture – where is the ground receptive to new concepts and new ideas of growth? What work needs to be done to ready the culture for new growth?

Where is the best place to grow something new – in an old bed of an existing brand or a new one? What kind of nutrients does it take? Give it the sun of attention or the shade of a skunk works? Should we plant a few first and see how it reacts to the environment – hold a pilot in a representative store?

Then, look though the eyes of **The Poet,** the root word of which is "poiesis," which means "to make." The tools of poetry and the charge to explore possibilities, deal with multiple drafts, iterate relentlessly on this relentless quest for the truth and for creating real value and delight for consumers.

After stealing lightning from the gods of inspiration as poets, it is time to see like **The Designer**, the ones who craft objects into indelible experiences, optimizing crude prototypes into desired iterations of wonder, beauty and sublime functionality.

At this point, the time has come to re-enter the lens of **The Consumer** again. As you move through rounds of co-creation of the prototypes, you can plug into the how much consumers or customers will desire your products or services, and learn what they may change to improve them.

To re-enter the enterprise, apply the eyes of **The Business**. You have already seen through most of the lens of the prism that are necessary to generate new value. You know what the market desires.

Now, apply an analytic overlay and figure out costs, go-to-market plans, and sell the portfolio of concepts to internal stakeholders. Why does it matter to the organization? How does it help us in the short and long term?

Without looking through a variety of lenses, an innovation can be pitifully myopic. By ensuring such projects look through various perspectives as part of the process, the chances of launching, market acceptance and market penetration are much greater.

Blind Spots,
Objective Leadership & the Dead

" *Once in a while you get shown the light/In the strangest of places/If you look at it right*" – *The Grateful Dead*

To celebrate the iconic lifestyle brand of the Grateful Dead and their recent sold out 50th anniversary reunion stadium run, let's talk about vision and its shadow side, blind spots.

Vision allows organizations the most competitive, legal advantage, perspective – perspective on the market, cultural and economic trends, and on itself. Perspective is the most rare and rarified tools of great leaders. The ability to see issues from every possible side, like lenses in a prism, allows objectivity on issues that defy habit, compulsion and fear.

Real vision is both visionary and pragmatic. While you survey the range of possible approaches, you scan for the most winning and advantageous opportunity with full knowledge of the risks and rewards.

Think of this level of leadership vision as being fully conscious. Such leaders are too rare. In fact, you can name them there are so few, the brave women and men who start movements, change the way we live for the better and create or leapfrog an industry.

This type of leadership can be trained and is achievable, but most do not want to endure the rigors of such intellectual honesty, emotional vulnerability and ardor. Instead, the majority of leaders never reach their potential. As a result, their organizations do not thrive as optimally as possible. So, they temper their vision and constrain the vision of those who work for them. After all, it is more comfortable to ignore blind spots and maintain tunnel vision than it is to see things as they are today and how they could be in the near future.

Perspective and objectivity are hard, hard work. Without an intention to be the best or a driving, demanding culture like the military, few answer their call to greatness. Instead, they waste time answering emails in meetings they didn't need to attend, a perfect place to hide, complete with a cloak of busyness.

By extending vision as a metaphor, we can look at common eyesight problems and infer organizational shortcomings, a lack of authentic leadership and tensions within a culture.

Tunnel Vision: Reduction in vision may be called tunnel vision, which aptly describes the problem. The image is clear in the center of the visual field, but the outer edges of the range of vision are blurry.

Hemianopia: With hemianopia, half the field of vision is blacked out in both the eyes. There is no treatment, either medical or surgical, for improving this condition, but sometimes it improves on its own with time. Field-expanding prism lens glasses and magnifiers may help.

Blind Spots: A blind spot is an area of the visual field that is obscure.

I'll leave the reader to connect the dots about which optic metaphor may fit the leadership of their organization, both the diagnosis and the prognosis. Know this, however, if your leaders have vision and objectivity, and can look at issues from many points of view, count your lucky stars, and be grateful you can see them.

What I Tell My Team.

Ask the hard questions.

As a thriving consultancy, our primary vocation is providing insight and objectivity that adds value to our clients. To meet this objective we have to play enlightened court jester, so to speak, asking all the un-askable questions those inside the company cannot ask. We also have to set the stage, carefully constructing an atmosphere of trust where we can mine issues deeply, uncover hidden orthodoxies, serve as a mirror, and always, always, always, point out reachable possibilities for growth. We also have a duty to name the obstacles. Asking the hardest questions about obstacles to growth and delivering the findings takes you deep inside the people who make up the culture. Sometimes there are "family style" secrets inside companies and walls of denial as thick as prison walls. Keep asking until you get to the heart of truth. Be respectful on this quest. People, especially tough people, are really tender.

Stay away from their politics.

Court jesters have the uncanny ability to speak of matters no one else in the system can touch. They stay free of political hairballs. They don't take sides. To play court jester well you need to have an innate mix of wisdom and whimsy. You also must have such strong conviction that you are not swayed or influenced by their organization's politics. Stay above that fray, even if well-intended people try to hip you to the pitfalls, personalities, and power struggles of that institution. This is their mountain to climb, not ours. By agreeing to trek it, we do not do our best work. Thank them, but do not engage. Do not touch that tar baby. Ultimately, we are paid for objectivity, which stays clear of the pollution of their politics. If we aren't free to express the truth in a diplomatic manner, the results will be compromised. If our client-side advocate doesn't have the requisite authority, it will just be a frustrating endeavor. Not worth the headache. Life, friends, is too short and there are other clients who sincerely value candor and the growth process.

Assume full authority.

While clients want insights and objectivity, what we really provide is courage, the courage to take calculated risks. To imbue this spirit of courage, we must radiate a genuine confidence. Confidence does not mean knowing things you don't know or having answers. Rather, confidence means that we assume full authority of the process and the results. Almost unconsciously, people inherently trust others who take full responsibility for their work. We are hired to make a difference, to find areas of growth where the company has not been able to do on its own. This exploration calls for different eyes, different experiences, and different mindsets that created the situation. Do not waste time trying to be like them or trying to fit it; this is not a playground. We are here to teach them to play for real, in the market by challenging themselves. Therefore, be your best self; that is why you are here.

Set and reenforce clear boundaries.

Sometimes clients get pressure and they transfer the pressure they receive onto you. Do not accept it. Keep your eye on the main goals and objectives. The best thing you can do for them is to stay focused on the tasks and process at hand. When this pressure strikes, they may ask you to work longer hours, respond to emails or calls in the middle of the night. Suffice to say, they begin to treat you like a vendor instead of a trusted consultant. Be polite, but politely refuse these distractions, gently reminding them of the main goal. As the old gospel song says, "keep your eye on the sparrow." Setting and maintaining boundaries is hard work, but necessary to create maximum value. Most often, these boundaries are threatened when clients are trying to subtly persuade you to engage in their politics, that proverbial mountain that you have no business climbing. Stay on the narrow road and refuse this detour with a firm but polite "no thank you; here's what I will do."

Trust the process.

Growth strategy and innovation are wayfinding processes. The insights and answers always emerge. Some anxious clients want previews and sneak peaks at time when, simply said, there is nothing real to show, just a bunch of theories and models of possibilities. If we were to share and they liked one of these strategies, it creates a problem because at this point everything is subject to change based on the progressive learning built into the process. Perhaps we have modeled out a solution but not yet finished testing market desirability? The client loves it and then the market won't accept it. Now, that is a sticky situation. Better to avoid these types of entanglements by just pointing to the point of the process where we are, inviting them into the somewhat messy process, but not distilling results before the wine of possibility has fermented.

The Corporate Inquisition of Intuition

While there are clear benefits of data and analytics when applied to growth efforts, a widespread, unhealthy dependence on a purely analytical approach to business cripples too many corporations.

While small- and mid-sized organizations still welcome some calculated risks backed by and bet on a team of spirited rising leaders, corporations appear more risk averse to their approach to launching new products in the market. In fact, the gestalt is that **we've entered a second age of enlightenment where nothing gets signed into action unless analytic models, predictive tools, and others first bless it with a numerical score.**

Note that these tools, while helpful, base their judgment on risk-averse human inputs; as well, they seek to envision a future outcome by using a snapshot of the present or past. While this theory may work in accurately forecasting some aspects of the future by looking at past behavior, which is the theoretical basis of a credit score, many market categories do not fit into this paradigm.

Other than a handful of renegade and famous exceptions who lead by their intuition – Steve Jobs, Iger of Disney, Juszkiewicz of Gibson Musical Instruments – global corporate culture distrusts leaders who rely on more intuitive decision making. This theme runs so strong, and cultural bias is so much in the favor of data and analytical types, that you could call this era of global business the witch hunt of intuitive types.

Call it the *corporate inquisition of intuition*. From board meetings to executive retreats to project-based huddles, **we see chart after chart imported straight off a dashboard, too often without human interpretation or in-depth critical thinking. The clear unspoken rule of this ubiquitous, prevalent trend is that God is a computer to be trusted implicitly and unthinkingly.**

What gets lost in this data-drunk era? The impetus to take risks. The will to take a stand and lead. The heart of creativity that drives culture forward.

And an engaged sense of the fullness of our humanity in the workplace.

Need proof? Ask any marketer. Here's one: David Roman, senior vice president and chief marketing officer of Lenovo, cautioned that there is a risk of becoming too enamored with data: "The risk is that we get so caught up in data and the analysis of it that we lose sight of the ultimate objective." The idea of a whole mind — right- and left-brain, analytical and creative, analogue and digital — needs a resurgence in the global world of business. Data can present facts in new patterns, but outside of cost-cutting big data hasn't lived up to the hype. Data equals information, not actionable insight, not wisdom. Yet, we have become addicted to the false assurance of data in too many areas where it shouldn't be applied.

Anyone making the case for new products or services, innovation, or marketing knows how monolithic a corporation can be and how biased it can be against some of the key growth levers like strategic thinking, customer experience, and intuition. **Some branches of business require both art and science — let's learn to value the art side of the equation.**

Why Hesitate?
Innovate. Start, and Learn.

Often there is so much anxiety about innovation. Is it just a fad, or is it a viable, potent form of value generation?

Is it something that needs to be outsourced, set up as a skunk works, or can I add it to the existing responsibilities of our employees?

Other companies are out-innovating us. The world has changed. Our market has changed. We claim that innovation is one of our core principles, a pillar, but the only program we tried was an idea-generation submission and it bloated our new product development pipeline.

We hear similar words in the echo chamber and water coolers of most corporate conversations of companies who have not yet figured out how to have a formal innovation program in their culture.

Getting started is the hardest part. So much time gets lost trying to predict the outcome before beginning the work – and with this type of work, front-end market exploration, predictions will not be accurate until you are knee-deep inside the process of a real project. Fretting at the starting line will not accelerate growth.

Innovation is not a linear, analytic process where a business case is built, investments made and products launched. Rather, it is a recursive, iterate framework for spending small increments of time and money to learn more and design a solution for a real problem.

The good news is that you can manage the budget carefully and get a staggering return on investment. The bad news is you have to adapt to a new work mode – and this point is where people get paralyzed before the work even starts.

Every possible excuse gets thrown up as a smokescreen from trying something new.

We need to fix our new-product development process first. We need to reorganize our sales organization first. We need to fix a few things in the culture first. We need to (fill in the blank with today's diversion).

Allow me to say that doing the front-end innovation work itself is curative, revealing so much about a company. You'll learn so much about the market, your team, your organizational structure and, most important, where to place and not place bets on growth.

You'll also figure out who are the team players, the big thinkers and the equally valuable detail doers. You'll stumble into unconscious defaults, blind spots, biases and obstacles inherent in the system of the organization. You'll learn deeply, but you have to start the process to earn these boons.

Admittedly, there is a driving bias toward action. Action stimulates. Action learns on its feet. Action engages people. Action connects companies with their customers in deep, meaningful ways. Action wins in a competitive marketplace. Action is contagious. Action helps retain high performers.

So, why are you reading this piece? You could be active, learning how to generate value that grows. Why hesitate? Innovate now. It's inexpensive to begin and might catalyze your organization for generations to come, but, as a sign reads in Las Vegas, "You must play to win."

About the Author

Michael Graber is the founder and managing partner of the Southern Growth Studio, an innovation + strategy boutique in Memphis. Michael publishes, speaks, and presents workshops on Innovation, Corporate Culture, Creativity, Business Model Strategy, and Leadership. For more, visit www.southerngrowthstudio.com